'The Color of the Skin Doesn't Matter'

'The Color of the Skin Doesn't Matter'

A Missioner's Tale of Faith and Politics in Africa

Janice McLaughlin, MM

ORBIS BOOKS
Maryknoll, New York 10545

Original publisher: Weaver Press, Box A1922, Avondale, Harare, Zimbabwe

North American edition published by Orbis Books, Box 302, Maryknoll, NY 10545-0302.

The title was inspired by the late Commander Josiah Tongogara (1938-79)

The majority of the photographs, many taken herself, are from Sister Janice's personal archive. Others are drawn from the Maryknoll Archive in New York. Grateful thanks are due to Stephanie Conning and Jennifer Halloran for their support. Dates and photographers are provided when these are known. Cover photograph, *The Rhodesia Herald*, 22 September 1977.

Manufactured in the United States of America

Library of Congress Control Number: 2021942378
ISBN 9781626984462 (paper)
ISBN 9781608339099 (ebook)

Contents

Acronyms

AACC	All Africa Conference of Churches (Nairobi)
ACOA	American Committee on Africa
AFCAST	Africa Forum for Catholic Social Teaching
CCJP	Catholic Commission for Justice and Peace
CCR	Centre for Conflict Resolution (Cape Town)
CIDSE	Cooperation Internationale pour le Development et la Solidarité
CIIR	Catholic Institute for International Relations (London)
ESAP	Economic Structural Adjustment Program
FRELIMO	Front for the Liberation of Mozambique
IHM	Immaculate Heart of Mary Sisters
LCBL	Little Children of our Blessed Lady
LCWR	Leadership Conference for Women Religious (USA)
MOGC	Maryknoll Office for Global Concern
NCCK	National Christian Council of Kenya
OCCZIM	Organization of Collective Cooperatives in Zimbabwe
RENAMO	Mozambique National Resistance (Movement)
SND	Sisters of Notre Dame
TAMOFA	Tanzania Mozambique Friendship Association
UNHCR	United Nations High Commission for Refugees
USCMA	United States Catholic Mission Association
WOA	Washington Office on Africa
ZANLA	Zimbabwe African National Liberation Army
ZANU	Zimbabwe African National Union
ZAPU	Zimbabwe African People's Union
ZIMFEP	Zimbabwe Foundation for Education with Production
ZIMOFA	Zimbabwe Mozambique Friendship Association
ZIPRA	Zimbabwe People's Revolutionary Army

Acknowledgements

Thanks are due to a number of people who helped these memoirs see the light of day. First, members of my Maryknoll community, too many to mention, who inspired me to take the 'road less travelled' and encouraged me when dark moments clouded my enthusiasm. Fay Chung shared so much with me in the camps in Mozambique and through all the years since. All the members of the Justice and Peace Commission in Zimbabwe who stood by me when I was arrested and imprisoned. These include Dieter Scholz, who later became a bishop, Fidelis Mukonori, who later became a priest and Geoff Feltoe. Others are no longer with us; Brother Arthur Dupuis and Mr John Deary. Justice Nick McNally, who died this year (2021) was a pillar of support and wise advice. Kathy Bond Stewart shared with me her passion for non-formal education and has inspired and supported me in many ways. Arkmore Kori, with whom I worked at Silveira House, added some paragraphs about our research work together. I am grateful to Srs Stephanie Conning and Jennifer Halloran helped me to identify photographs in the Maryknoll archive. Joseph Woods and David Harold Barry have generously edited my text and Irene Staunton and Murray McCartney of Weaver Press have seen the memoir through its final stages. To them all and many others not here included I would like to express my sincere thanks.

Janice McLaughlin, MM
Maryknoll, New York
February 2021

Foreword

As the final stages of editing this memoir were reached, news came of Janice's death on March 7, 2021, at Maryknoll, New York. Despite her increasing weakness over the past six months, she had followed the progress of this editing and had this foreword read to her not long before she died. She was pleased with it. I write this paragraph on the day of her funeral. There have been many tributes, among them from the President of Zimbabwe, Emmerson Mnangagwa, who knew Janice in Mozambique during the war.

***

The word 'missionary' is going out of fashion today. We have discovered that we are all missionaries to one another in some sense. Yet, the traditional use of the word still applies, for a little longer, to religiously motivated people who leave their own country to spend their lives in another where they render service in pastoral ministry, teaching in schools or universities or in nursing and medical work. Sr Janice McLaughlin, from the New York based Maryknoll Congregation of Sisters, was a 'missionary' in Africa but not in any of these ways.

Missionaries, in the sense of servants of the mission of Jesus to the world, are motivated by faith in him and in God's plan for humanity but from the 1960s this motivation often expressed itself in a struggle for justice. The Jesuits, for example, explicitly linked proclamation of the faith with the struggle for justice in their 1974 meeting in Rome. From the moment Janice arrived in Tanzania in 1969 this desire to contribute to the promotion of justice was the driving force of her life. Her entry point into this mission was through journalism, both teaching it and practicing it.

Reading her memoir, one is astonished at her courage in becoming engaged in issue after issue without seeming to hesitate.

At one point she tells us she might agonize for days over what dress to wear at some function but for life-changing decisions, which were often risky and dangerous, she did not hesitate. By her own admission she was careless about her own safety. She left incriminating evidence lying around when she was in Rhodesia and later expressed horror when she reflected how her diary was read out in court and her negligence implicated others. But it was all an expression of her generous self-giving without 'counting the cost'.

The intensity and depth of feeling she had for her mission, which is described in these pages, is a measure of the generosity of her commitment to the struggle for freedom and independence for Zimbabwe. This book also shows the variety of initiatives in which Janice was involved and where she was often among the prime movers. For a short while, at the time of her imprisonment and deportation in 1977, she was an international celebrity but she understood the ephemeral nature of this publicity and quickly returned to Africa and entered into the raw life of the refugee camps. Before and after Independence in Zimbabwe (1980) she worked to bring education to the refugees and displaced people both in Mozambique and later in Zimbabwe.

She wrote articles and gave talks on what was happening in the lives of ordinary people as a result of the liberation war and the civil disturbances that followed in both Mozambique and Zimbabwe after independence in both countries. She did a major study, *On the Frontline*,[1] on the effects of the liberation war on four missions in remote rural areas of Zimbabwe.

Her desire to be 'with the people' was not a romantic armchair wish; she actually lived in a small house with another Maryknoll sister in Tafara, a 'high density' low-income suburb of Harare, for four years before being recalled to New York to work in the

---

1   *On the Frontline: Catholic Missions in Zimbabwe's Liberation War.* Baobab Books: Harare, 1996.

media and later to be President, that is, over all responsible, for the worldwide Maryknoll community. Her heart was always in Africa and at the end of her term she returned to work as a facilitator and animator in training courses for advocacy and peace building in Zimbabwe. Among the many causes she took up in these later years was the exploitation and trafficking of woman.

This memoir reveals a generous heart and an attentive mind. Janice shares with us her reflections on what she sees as the new role of the Church in the modern world. While rooted in her Catholic faith and her Maryknoll religious family she does not hesitate to express her frustration at the slow pace of the Catholic Church in welcoming women into decision making and administration. This is not a struggle for recognition of women for their own sake but for the sake of the Church which is missing out because it finds it so difficult to move forward and slough off the weight of tradition.

Janice tells us she had many heroes; Julius Nyerere, Josiah Tongogara, as well as her own Maryknoll sisters who gave their lives in El Salvador. One person who deeply impressed her was Bishop Mandlenkosi Zwane of Eswatini and she quotes him in her book, *On the Frontline*: 'My fear is that the Church will not be in a position to minister in a revolutionary situation … It is because of our attitude, because of our historical background, because of all kinds of things that have happened to us. We are imprisoned … We only want to reform things, not radically change them. None of us is prepared for radical change. That is my fear.'[2]

That Janice could put this quotation at the head of the Epilogue of her book suggests that the bishop expresses something she holds dearly. She was prepared to be a called a revolutionary and a radical and her memoir shows how she tried to live this attitude all her life. She would be the first to admit that in some ways she was naive but she struck out ahead of others to blaze a trail even if

---

2   Ibid.

she was not sure where it would lead or who would follow.

Like many who had struggled and longed for the liberation of Zimbabwe, Janice was disillusioned by the way the new government of Zimbabwe was content to 'enjoy the fruits' of freedom without addressing the fundamental structures which continued to frustrate the aspirations of the people. The massive struggle that had taken around 60,000 lives ended with the replacement of one set of rulers, the whites, with another, the blacks. Nothing fundamental to the lives of the majority changed. Janice wrote her memoir forty years after the freedom she gave so much for was attained. But it was only a partial freedom. Sadly, another revolution, hopefully peaceful this time, will be needed if all the people are to enjoy the fruits of their hard-won independence.

Dieter B. Scholz SJ
Emeritus Bishop of Chinhoyi
Harare, 16 February 2021

Preface

When I was writing this personal memoir, families and friends of a young black men killed by the police in the United States launched the 'Black Lives Matter' campaign to draw attention to the racism prevalent among some members of the police and to demand accountability. The brutal murder – on camera – of George Floyd by a police officer on the 25 May 2020 in Minneapolis was a painful reminder to America and the wider world, of racism within the ranks of the police force.

So, I am aware that skin color not only matters but can mean the difference between life and death. Racism, and other prejudicial attitudes, divide human beings and can even lead to war, as happened in white-ruled Rhodesia where much of this memoir takes place.

Having lived more than half of my life in black-ruled Africa, I know well the privileges my white skin has afforded me. I witnessed firsthand the indignities black people suffer. I had seen this in my native United States and now I witnessed it in Rhodesia and via apartheid in South Africa. These indignities did not end with the coming of majority rule but endured in all the countries of southern Africa where I lived and they continue to do so in my home country of America. Add to this mix, crippling poverty and an internalized sense of inferiority and both are common to both parts of my world.

The title of this memoir, therefore, expresses an ideal, a dream of a society without barriers to achievement; a society where racism, sexism, classism and other forms of prejudice which divide us is abolished. Speaking of South Africa after the defeat of apartheid in 1994, Archbishop Desmond Tutu coined the expression, 'the rainbow people of God'. He was expressing a vision of a society without racial discrimination and without privileges or punishments based on race alone.

South African freedom fighter and later chief justice Albie Sachs held a similar vision. 'Black is Beautiful, Brown is Beautiful, White is Beautiful', he declared.[3] He went on to explain: 'That is what we want, in South Africa, everywhere in the world. White made itself ugly by declaring that black was ugly. Now ironically, it is black that will help white discover the beauty in itself.'

These are noble sentiments. I experienced a foretaste of this when I worked with the Zimbabwe Project in Mozambique during the final years of the liberation war in Rhodesia. Every person I met in the Zimbabwe African National Union (ZANU) party led by Robert Mugabe, from the leaders to the young men and women fighters, treated me with kindness and respect. They laughed at my American idiosyncrasies, such as my habit of saving a portion of my food to eat the following day in case there would be nothing, which was often the case: 'How will you feel when you are the only one eating?' They taught me to live in the present and appreciate the small pleasures of each day – a piece of sugarcane, a bucket of warm water for bathing, a sliver of soap. All were precious and unexpected in the camps where food and every other necessity was scarce.

Yet the color of my skin, my American nationality and my religious vocation mattered a great deal to them. 'They will listen to you,' a ZANU supporter told me when he invited me to give talks on college campuses in the United States. My race, nationality, sex and religion were also an asset to the liberation forces based in Mozambique where I readily agreed to give radio and newspaper interviews supporting the goals of the struggle. I was aware that I would be criticized by some for taking sides but I did not believe that neutrality was an option. These pages will help to explain

3   Towards a Rainbow Nation in a United South Africa, Dept. of Law, University of Cape Town. 1991.

how I reached that decision.

I had reservations about writing this memoir. My life is no more important than any other but I happened to be there with Zimbabweans at that moment of their history. I also wondered if I would be seen as glorifying the liberation war. In a right-wing book that came out before Independence I was called 'a cheer-leader for the terrorists'. 'Terrorist' was a word used by the Rhodesians for the African people who rose against them. This memoir is a personal account of how I experienced events and must stand as such.

I may also be seen as glorifying the Catholic Church by glossing over its faults, such as male dominance and the failure to give women leadership roles as well as the handling of the scandal of sex abuse among its members. My traditional Catholic upbringing may have blinded me to these things. Although I have embraced new theologies and ways of being a Christian, I find spiritual nourishment in the ancient rituals and prayer. Scripture and especially the psalms have sustained me throughout difficult challenges.

At the approach of my 80th birthday, I look back with deep appreciation on those who formed me, especially the Maryknoll Sisters who gave me the freedom and the encouragement to be a global pilgrim. Some mentors will be mentioned in these pages while others live on in my memory and in the litany of the saints who have graced my life.

Sister Janice McLaughlin
(Photo: Archive – Maryknoll Sisters)

1

Introduction

'General Tongogara would like to meet you.' I was startled by this message having heard of the legendary figure and head of ZANU's army, and having seen his photo in magazines and newspapers but I never expected to meet him in person. I was in the VIP lounge at the airport in Maputo, waiting for a flight to the north of Mozambique.

A giant of a man entered the lounge and gave me a hug while he regarded me with flashing golden eyes like those of a lion. His gaze was probing, as if he could see into my innermost depths. His face broke into a smile lightening up the space around us. 'Thank you', he said, 'you helped us teach the comrades that the colour of the skin doesn't matter'. I was overwhelmed and humbled by this statement, coming from the commander of ZANU's liberation army. I had seen the division in white-ruled Rhodesia and had assumed white people would be considered enemies.

Tongogara went on to explain that the war was against the system, not against white people, and this was the message taught to freedom fighters in the camps and refugees who crossed to Mozambique. It was also the message at the *pungwes* or all-night meetings with the rural people inside Rhodesia. 'We tell the comrades the one who points a gun at us is the enemy and in most cases, it is our black brothers and sisters. We tell them many white people support our struggle – farmers, businessmen and priests. Now we have an example', he continued, 'we can point to you, Sister Janice, and say you went to prison and were deported because you supported us'. I was later to see, in the camps for Zimbabweans in the centre and north of Mozambique, posters with the same message declaring, 'The colour of the skin is not the enemy'.

We talked for several minutes as he recounted examples of Catholic priests who supported the guerrillas. 'We are fighting to change the system', he repeated, not to kill or expel white people'. I was overwhelmed not only by Tongogara's words but by his presence. The heat, dirt and stench in the airport faded before this imposing figure who exuded confidence and a sense of power. His smile was captivating and his manner of speaking clear and straightforward. I was young, impressionable and prone to hero worship. Tongogara was my romanticized version of some of the revolutionary leaders that I had read and studied in Kenya; he was Fidel Castro, Che Guevara and Amilcar Cabral rolled into one. I could picture him standing in front of the troops, exhorting them to risk their lives for the freedom of their country, giving them courage by his words and his personality. I felt somehow bigger and more confident just standing next to him.

He took me to meet his wife and his youngest son who had come to the airport to say good-bye to him as he was returning to the front. His wife, Angeline, and their son, Bvumai, the youngest of three, shyly greeted me. Two older sons, Hondo and Tichafa, were attending school. They never knew if they would see their father again each time he returned to the frontline.

Charles Ndlovu (whose real name was Webster Shamu), ZANU's Deputy Communications Director and who was one of those who introduced me to Tongo, as the general was called, snapped photos of us that ended up on election posters in 1980.

The year was 1978 and I was working in Mozambique for Zimbabwe Project, an initiative set up by Catholic aid agencies in Europe to assist refugees who had fled the fighting in Rhodesia as well as young people who had crossed the border to join the freedom fighters. Before coming to Mozambique, I worked in post-independent Kenya in the early 1970s and in Rhodesia at the end of that decade. Although I had grown up during the civil rights era in my own country and had participated in demonstrations against racism, I hadn't personally experienced what it meant. But now I encountered the inequality and racial divisions in Africa. As a white missionary in a black world, I had a lot to learn. General Tongogara and other Zimbabwean freedom fighters were my teachers as were Kenyan journalists, authors and other missionaries.

The following chapters trace the journey where I faced my ignorance, prejudices and the privileges I enjoyed. They also explore my empathy for those who suffer. It was a journey from my insular upbringing in a working-class neighborhood in Pittsburgh, Pennsylvania, to a religious community in the midst of radical change. Later I came to East Africa at a time of newly won freedom with the attendant need for social and economic transformation. Finally, I was set down in the middle of a war of liberation for equality and majority rule in Southern Rhodesia. These pages will follow the long and winding road, I took and the lessons that I learned along the way.

2

What's in a Name? Tracing my Roots

My mother named me Janice after a character in a novel. 'I just liked the sound of it', she told me. When I was old enough to read, she gave me a copy of the book, *Janice Meredith* by Paul Ford. My namesake lived during the American war of Independence from Britain. In this fictional account, she hid the freedom fighters and their weapons in her home and was a reliable supporter of George Washington and his forces. 'Your namesake must have influenced you to support the struggle for freedom in faraway Rhodesia', I was often told. I loved the story and my name.

My parents, Mary Louise Schaub and Paul Richard McLaughlin, came from different backgrounds and couldn't have been more opposite in upbringing, personality and outlook on life. My mother was very talkative, outgoing and fun loving. My father was quiet, hardworking and serious. She was a college graduate while my father never finished high school. She came from a large family and seemed prosperous while my father had only one sister and had been raised by a maiden aunt after his mother died when he was young. 'Schaub' means 'bundles of straw'. Her German ancestors were probably roofers who thatched houses throughout the area in Bavaria where they lived. One branch of the Schaub family immigrated to the United States in 1650 and settled in Pittsburgh.

On a visit to Ireland, I was told that McLaughlin, my father's surname, means son of a Viking. His father's family may have come from Donegal in the north-west of Ireland. The history of Ireland, like that of the African continent, is a tale of invasions and colonization. Even though he had never been to Ireland, my father was a staunch Irish nationalist who supported the liberation of Northern Ireland from British rule. This undoubtedly influenced my view of the British colonists in both Kenya and Rhodesia, where I later lived. In fact, it may have been one of the driving forces behind my passion for justice and concern for the poor and oppressed. That, and my perception of the inequality between my father and mother's families, made me a defender of the underdog.

My mother went to Frick Teacher's College, a branch of the University of Pittsburgh. She majored in physical education, which puzzled me since she was not very athletic. When I asked her about it much later, she said with a laugh, 'It was the easiest'. She was extremely intelligent and widely read but she would rather read, play bridge and go out with friends than spend time studying. Perhaps one of the most important things we learned from her was to enjoy life and treat ourselves to simple pleasures regardless of our outward circumstances. A cup of tea and a good book got me through many hard times in religious life and on the African continent.

My father was very gentle and kind with a dry sense of humor. He was quiet and let my mother, sister and me do most of the talking. He had a strong sense of justice and a concern for the poor that may have stemmed from his own experience. While he didn't talk much about his family, we learned little by little from his sister

Margie and from some of his aunts and uncles that his early life had been hard. His mother, Mary Connolly, who had come from Ireland when she was eighteen years old, married Francis Patrick McLaughlin in Pittsburgh five years later. They had four children, three girls and a boy. Mary died in the great flu epidemic of 1918 when her son Paul, the third born, was only five years old and she was only thirty-three. Two years later another tragedy struck the family. My father and his two older sisters, eight and ten at the time, were hit by a car when they were crossing a street near their home in a snowstorm. The two girls, Anna and Mary Frances, died from their injuries while my father survived.

After this tragedy, my father and his young sister Margaret, (Marge or Margie), moved in with their aunt, also called Margaret, whom they adored. The house also held several uncles as well as our aunt Mary who never married but helped Margaret look after this growing family. In order to support the family, my father dropped out of high school and got a job with a local builder. His income helped to put his sister Marge through school but deprived him of further education. My father never mentioned the hardships of his early life. I wonder now how the early death of his mother and the tragic accident that took the lives of his two older sisters and spared him may have influenced him. Perhaps it helps explain his attraction to my mother who brought excitement and laughter into his life.

Her first date with my father was at the ice-skating rink in Oakland. 'He was the only one I knew who had a car', she told me. 'I decided to trip and fall to see what he would do'. Paul helped her up and was concerned that she was wet and cold so he drove her home in his car. This was the start of their romance. My mother loved to tell the story of his proposal: 'We were walking through town after seeing a movie and stopped in front of Horne's Department Store where a bedroom set was displayed. 'Shall we get it for our home when we are married?' Paul asked. My mother thought he was joking but he said it again. 'I said "yes" and fifty years later I still have that bedroom set'.

Her parents were opposed to the marriage because of the huge difference in their upbringing and circumstances. Mary Louise prevailed and she and Paul were married at the parish church with her sister Ruth as the bridesmaid and Dan McMahon, a close friend, as best man. Her parent's misgivings lingered unspoken in the background and the gap between my parents grew deeper over time, though it never diminished the love and attention they gave to my sister and me.

I was born in 1942, several years after my parents were married. Three years later, my sister Mary Ellen appeared. She had curly red hair and a round chubby face. 'Is this my sister?' I wailed when they brought her home from the hospital. I was told that I would have a playmate and I expected her to be my age and size. I eventually recovered from my disappointment and became her protector and constant companion. 'I'm de mommy', I would declare as I watched over her.

My father was a traditional Irish husband who believed that a wife should stay home and look after the house and the children. Although my mother could have earned twice what he did by teaching, she accepted his demand. She didn't return to the classroom until we were grown up and had left home. I often wondered why she gave in to our father and what this had meant for her.

'I could never be myself', she confessed many years later. I was stunned and began to understand what a high price she paid for giving in to my father on many occasions. He expected her to be a good cook and housekeeper like the aunt who had raised him. My mother had been raised with a live-in cook and maid. She tried her best to be a good housewife but it was a strain. She passed her dislike of domesticity to my sister and me. 'I could have been a school principal like my friends', she later lamented. Because she felt like a failure in the kitchen, mom never taught us how to cook. We helped her with some of the cleaning but never found any joy in housework.

My sister and I became our mother's pupils and she devoted herself to our education. Not only did she instill a love of reading but she also introduced us to many sports and taught us how to swim and to play tennis. Mary Ellen and I looked forward to going with her to the library each week to withdraw three books that we would devour and exchange the following week for three more. Mom introduced us to the leading children's books – *Winnie the Pooh, The Wind in the Willows, Alice in Wonderland* and Hans Christian Anderson's book of fairy tales. We had a complete set of the illustrated Oz books as well as a children's book of Greek mythology. As we got older, she introduced us to the novels of Sigred Unset about the oppression of women as well as the Russian authors Tolstoy and Dostoevsky. We also read the lives of the saints. 'There is no Saint Janice so I will be the first one', I proclaimed with great pride.

Later our mother took us to art galleries, museums, concerts, ballets and the theater. Mary Ellen and I became ardent fans of the arts for the rest of our lives. One Thanksgiving when I was probably about twelve years old stands out; our father had gone hunting with his friends in the mountains of Pennsylvania, leaving us on one of the most important family holidays of the year. This infuriated my mother who decided to give us a rare treat. We went by train to New York, stayed in the Biltmore Hotel, ate in some of the best restaurants and went to the theater every night, seeing some of the current Broadway shows. My mother used the money she had inherited from her parents to give us this unforgettable experience. Even then, I recognized this as an act of rebellion on her part, full of creativity and resilience. Paul never left us again over the Thanksgiving holiday and my mother now paid for an annual vacation of two weeks each summer from her inheritance.

Our father found his outlet in nature. He was an outdoorsman and shared this love with us, his daughters. Mary Ellen and I planted vegetables with him each spring in a tiny garden in our backyard. We raked leaves with him in the fall and shoveled snow in the winter. Best of all, he took us fishing with him on lakes and rivers in Pennsylvania. Sitting quietly for hours in a boat, waiting for the fish to bite, was probably my first experience of contemplative prayer. Suspended between the blue water of the lake and the cloudless sky above, I floated on an inner journey to a father God who I believed lived on a cloud in the sky, being serenaded by choirs of angels and looking down on me. I found this image very consoling at the time and was mesmerized by the patterns of clouds in the sky.

My father was good with his hands and knew every aspect of construction such as plumbing, painting, electrical work, roofing and brick-laying. I wish that I had paid more attention to the work my father did and had learned to take care of simple repairs and maintenance of a house and car. Instead, I followed in my mother's footsteps and always had my nose in a book, expecting that my father or someone equally handy would take care of any problem that arose. Lucky for me, they usually did!

One of my earliest memories is of the igloo that my father built for me in our background after a big snowfall. He fashioned the snow into bricks and placed them together to create a round dome that was high enough for me to enter and sit upright. It was surprisingly warm inside this ice-house. The sun shining through the frozen snow created a pattern of sparkling shapes. I felt as if I was in my own private castle and spent hours playing inside my secret hideaway. I never minded being alone and created other secret places where I would play with my dolls and other toys without any interruption. The igloo became a symbol for me of the solitude and silence that I craved throughout my active and eventful life.

I was not always a hermit, however, and liked to stage performances for my parents and neighbors to watch. I also imitated life with my sister in games that I made up like 'office', 'home' and 'church'. Bishop McDowell, the auxiliary bishop of Pittsburgh whose mother lived on our street, saw me playing church one day. 'She's sure to be a priest', he jokingly told my parents. 'She took up a collection after the sermon'.

Our life was not always easy. 'You grew up poor', a cousin once reminded me. It was true that we did not have much money and learned to live with the basic necessities but I never felt poor. Although we lived simply and were careful about spending, we had a house, a car and went on two-week vacations every year. We received a first-rate education at the parish school where the Dominican Sisters from Columbus, Ohio, now Sisters of Peace, taught us from Grade One through high school. It's true that my father, who never finished high school, received a minimum wage as a pump repairman and did not play golf or belong to a country club like most of my mother's family. In fact, he refused to set foot in a country club but he did not prevent my sister and me from joining our cousins for a swim and a meal there.

Our father's work as a pump repairman took him to steel mills and coal mines. Over supper he would tell us about the dangers that the workers faced, their poor working conditions and low pay. He became a staunch believer in unions and the need for workers to unite. He joined his workmates in a strike against the owners of Harris Pump and Supply Company where he worked. The fact that the husband of a great-aunt was the head of the company made this act even more heroic in our eyes. The workers lost and our uncle declared it a union-free zone. Our father stayed on in order to support his family but took no satisfaction in the job.

We lived in an ethnic, working-class neighborhood in Pittsburgh's East End where Irish, Italian and Germans lived side by side. Pittsburgh was a city of immigrants who came to work in the steel mills that lined the banks of the three rivers. Many of my relatives on my father's side of the family worked in the steel mills and it is most likely that his father, who was a welder, did so as well. An African American community lived on the hill not far from the church and school that I attended. We rarely saw them as they had their own churches and stores and attended the public school since they were not Catholic. I don't recall ever being told anything negative about people of different races and nationalities but our paths rarely crossed. It was probably a form of segregation but it seemed normal for us to live in neighborhoods with people like ourselves.

We lived on the ground floor of a three-story brick house that my father had bought with a mortgage from the bank. He rented out the top two floors to tenants who stayed with us for many years because of the low rent that he charged as well as the upkeep and maintenance that my father provided. Coincidentally our house was next door to the house where my father was raised and was within walking distance of the home of my mother's parents that was only a block from our school.

I loved school and enjoyed competition; I was not happy if I came in second. Through the first eight grades, I competed with a boy in the class to be number one. He was a neighbor as well as a friend. I took him to my senior prom and we have remained friends over the years. 'Could I have married him?' I sometimes wondered as I saw my classmates marry their high school sweet hearts. But I knew from a very young age that I wanted something more than taking care of a house and children.

Spelling bees, debates and public speaking gave me confidence in public and may have been the reason that I was elected as the student leader in high school. I was also athletic and played on the basketball team, winning several trophies. There were only thirty-two of us in our high school class and we formed lasting friendships that have sustained me over the years.

When my parents quarreled, it was usually about money. My mother always wanted more and my father was content with what we had. 'You only need two sets of clothes – one to wear while the other is being washed', our father often told us as he surveyed our crowded closets. Our mother, on the other hand, loved to shop and to wear the latest fashions. We never bought anything that wasn't in a sale, however. Each spring and fall we would take the bus to the department stores in town to get the best prices for our school and summer outfits. Even now I always look at price tags and usually buy the least expensive item. I welcome the hand-me-downs from my aunt and my cousins who can afford the best. I admired my father's ability to do without but my sister and I took after our mother! We loved to shop and to wear the beautiful dresses that our aunts made for us. Later in life my father would tease me: 'You took the vow of poverty but I live it'. There was more than a little truth to those words.

There were members of religious communities on my mother's side of the family. Although I never met them, I heard about them and knew they were much admired and respected. An uncle, Andrew Schaub, was a diocesan priest in Pittsburgh and an aunt, Mother Jerome Schaub, was the founder of a community of Ursuline Sisters in Paola, Kansas. I learned through her obituary that we shared a love of nature and an interest in reading, especially mystery stories. I doubt if the knowledge of these relatives influenced my decision to become a religious but I was happy to learn about them and proud that I was related to them.

My idea of God was probably shaped by artwork in the books of saints that I read. I pictured God, as mentioned above, as an old man with a long beard seated on a throne in the clouds while being serenaded by choirs of angels. I would spend hours lying on my back looking up at the sky and seeing images of animals in the clouds. Usually there were rays of light coming from a single cloud that I imagined was God's home. I did not question this image of an old white man in the sky until many years later. In fact, I found it comforting to think of God watching over me from above. I was fascinated by nature for as long as I can remember. I squatted for hours watching ants carrying grains of sand and dirt into their underground tunnels and imagining the streets and alleys that they were constructing down there. We had a cat named Pepper that used to fight with the dogs in the neighborhood. He died from a gash in his neck from one of these fights, leaving me inconsolable. I held an elaborate funeral for Pepper and did the same for dead birds and mice. All were like friends to me and I mourned their passing with tears and religious rituals. Later in life, the cutting down of trees and the destruction of forests were as emotionally upsetting as the death of elephants and rhino's and I mourned the killing of whales and the death of coral reefs. Nature connected me to a Creator God and has remained a constant in my life.

Our parents taught my sister and me not to discriminate against people but to treat everyone the same. My mother was a master at this, making friends with everyone she met – the mailman, grocer, butcher, the stranger sitting next to her on the bus. She was genuinely interested in every person she met and they opened up and shared their life stories with her. This embarrassed Mary Ellen and me and we used to stand or sit as far away from her as possible and pretend that we didn't know her. Ironically, I find myself acting like my mother now, speaking to strangers and being fascinated by each one's unique life story.

After school we played games with the children in the neighborhood before we came in to do our homework. My favorite game was hide-and-seek. I took great delight in finding very unique hiding places where I was seldom found. Once when some cousins came to visit, we played in our basement, which was very spooky with many dark corners to hide. I climbed into an empty trunk, sure that I would never be found. I stayed there for what seemed like hours until I decided that it was safe to come out and claim my victory. When I tried to open the lid, however, it wouldn't budge. I lay back down, waiting for someone to come and rescue me. I was getting sleepy from lack of air when a small glimmer of light shone through the lid. I shouted, 'Help, help' as loud as I could. When the light went off again, leaving me in total darkness with little possibility to escape, I resigned myself to a slow death by suffocation inside the trunk. I wasn't afraid but felt that God was holding me and that I would fall gently to sleep and wake up in heaven. Soon a light went on again and the lid of the trunk was lifted up. My father stood there with tears streaming down his face. I had been missing for several hours and my cousins had all gone home, thinking I was playing a joke on them. Dad pulled me out and carried me up the stairs. 'I didn't hear you calling', he said, 'but something made me go back to the basement and open the trunk'.

This was the first of several close calls over the years. Perhaps this experience influenced me more than I realized at the time. Although I shy away from outward displays of fervor or religious sentimentalism, I have never doubted that God is with me and am confident that I will be rescued from any danger.

3

A Dream Come True:
The Long Road to Africa

I wanted to be a missionary in Africa from as far back as I can remember. Perhaps I was influenced by the colorful photos of children from other countries in the *Maryknoll* magazine that my grandparents received. Maybe the Dominican Sisters of Columbus, Ohio, who taught me at St Lawrence O'Toole grade and high school, planted the seed of my vocation.

I often joke that I credit my vocation to Sister Mary Gerald, a fourth-grade teacher who gave me a punishment for talking during class. I was obliged to copy a page from our geography book one hundred times. That particular page had a full-color, two-page spread of elephants, giraffes, zebras and wildebeests grazing at the foot of Mount Kilimanjaro in East Africa. 'One day I will see this in person', I vowed as I copied the words on the page.

Whatever the cause, I never deviated or doubted this call to be a missioner. When I made my first communion in third grade, one of the nuns suggested that my white veil was so beautiful that I should keep it for my wedding. I am told that I responded very forcefully: 'I am not going to get married. I'm going to be a missionary in Africa'.

No one was surprised, therefore, when in high school I started exploring different communities. In my junior year, Sr Maria del Rey, a journalist and well-known author who hailed from Pittsburgh, came to a local department store on a book signing tour. My mother and I attended the event and invited her and her companion to our home for lunch.

Over the meal, I learned more about the Maryknoll Sisters, the community to which they belonged, and resolved to write to the Vocation Director, explaining my interest. I was invited to the Maryknoll Sisters' Center in Ossining, New York, for an interview in my senior year of high school. My mother accompanied me as far as New York City. 'You're on your own now', she said as she watched me board the train for Ossining at Grand Central Station. I was filled with excitement during the one-hour ride along the Hudson River, sure that I would soon see my dream fulfilled.

I returned to the city that evening very crestfallen. Sr Rose Agnes, the Vocation Director, rejected me. She asked many questions and then said. 'Get a job, a boyfriend and go to college'. I was shocked. I was sure they would snatch me up on my first try! I came from a reasonably devout Catholic family. My mother, sister and I went to daily Mass in Advent and Lent. We prayed the rosary each evening on our knees in our parents' bedroom to the dramatic voice of Bishop Fulton Sheen. I was an all-A student and head of the Student Council. I was also a member of our award-winning basketball team and debating team. Wasn't I a perfect candidate for religious life?

On the other hand, I was stubborn and also somewhat rebellious. If I was told to do something that I didn't want to do, I simply ignored the order. I was often sent to bed without my supper to teach me to obey. The lesson never sunk in and I continued to go my own way, annoying my parents and delighting my classmates and friends who thought I was very brave. 'You were a dare-devil', a cousin told me. 'You used to sled down the steepest hills and dive off the highest boards. You did head stands and back flips, climbed onto roofs and over fences. We could hardly keep up with you'. I don't think I was so brave but it's true that I had no fear and liked to be the leader. My greatest pleasure was swinging as high as I could go on a rope swing affixed to a huge tree in our back yard. Once I swung so high that I went right over the top, making me a local hero for daring and taking risks. I figured that this trait was also a positive indicator that I should be a missionary, travelling to far-flung countries that were dangerous and where life could be uncomfortable.

Only later did I recognize the wisdom in the decision to wait before joining Maryknoll. I got my first job in the summer of my senior year, keeping inventory in a motor parts company. It was boring but I enjoyed the women with whom I worked and one of them set me up to date her brother. He took me to an outdoor movie, something that no longer exists. My mother warned me about the danger of going to a drive-in movie where young couples often went to make out under the cover of darkness. I was nervous on this first date but Dave was very polite and strictly hands off. We stopped at Eat 'N Park on our way home for a hamburger and milkshake and I felt like one of the gang. Now I could exchange stories with my classmates who often went there after a date.

When my date dropped me off at my front door, we shook hands politely and that was the end of that encounter. I probably scared him away by my nervousness and uncertainty about what to do. Although I had attended high school proms with boys from my former grade school class, I did not consider these excursions to be dates but a formality to be endured. I was so focused on becoming a missionary that I never considered the possibility of falling in love, getting married and having children, which was the dream of most of my classmates. Only much later in life did I begin to find men interesting and attractive. As a teen-ager in an all-girls' high school, they were far away from my life and imagination.

I had been awarded a scholarship to attend St Mary of the Springs College in Columbus, Ohio, that was run by the same Dominican community that taught me at St Lawrence O'Toole primary and secondary school. That September my parents drove me to the beautiful campus in a quiet corner of Columbus. This was my first time away from home and I was excited and also a little scared. I had never ventured far from home and from my small circle of friends who attended the same school, went to the same church, played the same games and probably shared the same views. In the dormitory at St Mary's, I shared a room with two other young women who may have been equally scared. They were both from Ohio and we became fast friends. I made many lifelong friends there and travelled all over the state of Ohio as a member of the volleyball team. I dated a student at Ohio State who took me to football games and wanted to take me home to meet his parents. He was not a Catholic and was puzzled when I told him I was going to join a religious community. I felt guilty that I hadn't told him sooner. I also had a crush on my Spanish teacher who was from Puerto Rico. Spanish became my favorite subject!

Toward the end of my first year of college in 1961, I wrote again to the Maryknoll Sisters' headquarters, asking them to admit me. Although Sr Rose Agnes encouraged me to complete four years of college, she eventually relented and said yes. At eighteen years of age, in September 1961, I joined the Maryknoll Sisters, the first American community of Catholic women religious founded exclusively for global mission. This was the first of many steps in my journey to the African continent. It would be another eight years before I arrived in East Africa in 1969 to begin language studies on the shores of Lake Victoria.

4

The Novitiate:
A Training Ground for Mission

I viewed the long years of training before I was sent overseas as a testing ground and preparation for the life on the missions. We began with nine months as 'postulants', that is, applicants being familiarized with the life before beginning the two-year program as novices. Our way of life was monastic and governed by rules: No talking after lights out at 9:00 p.m.; no talking in twos; no 'particular' or exclusive friendships; no phone calls, radio, newspaper or television. In other words, we were cut off from the external world and lived in a kind of medieval bubble.

We kept silence for all but one hour of each day and rose early in the morning for meditation and Mass. Not being an early riser, this was a huge effort for me. I took a cold shower each morning to wake me up but still fell asleep during the half hour of silent meditation. During the day we had classes in theology and scripture as well as anthropology and cultural studies. When we weren't in class, we were involved in manual labor. I was assigned to the sewing room where I learned to make our long habits or uniforms. We also scrubbed floors, cleaned toilets, washed dishes, pots and pans. I had grown up helping my mother with the housework so I was used to this though it wasn't something I enjoyed doing any more than my mother had. 'It's like a marine boot camp', a relative announced on hearing about the schedule. 'You either sink or swim'. I managed but sometimes wondered if it was worth the effort.

Some of the religious practices were strange. Each month we met to confess our faults to the group. At the end of our litany of small infractions of the rule such as breaking a glass or scorching a slip when ironing, each of us had to throw ourselves face down on the floor in a pose of contrition. Called the *venia*, this practice must have originated in medieval times and caused many of the young women in my group to develop knee and shoulder problems. These group confessions also caused a lot of hilarity and often had to be cancelled because we were laughing so much. We laughed during the reading of the stories of the ascetics and martyrs of the past with their bizarre penances and mortifications: sleeping on a bed of thorns or whipping themselves with nettles.

Our prayer life made much more sense. We recited the Divine Office in common three times a day. The poetry of the psalms and the chanting carried me to that safe place in the boat fishing with my father and sister. We also did spiritual reading from some of the ancient as well as more recent spiritual masters. I fell in love with the thought of Teilhard de Chardin although I didn't always understand what I was reading. I appreciated the reading of mission diaries during meals when we heard of the day-to-day life of the Sisters overseas. These tales of courage and everyday heroism whetted my desire to join these pioneers on the frontlines of the Church in remote and neglected places.

We also had fun! We went for hikes in the woods, played

basketball and other sports and most of all, we put on spectacular performances for sisters visiting from other places. I recall on one occasion decorating the auditorium to look like an Italian cafe with red and white checked table cloths, candles and a fountain in the middle of the room. We did modern dance and also marching drills, led by some of the members of our group. It was never boring and all talents were accepted and utilized. 'Simplicity nights', or what I would call amateur hours, were a Maryknoll tradition for feasts and special occasions. Each one was invited to contribute something – a song, poem, dance, joke – whatever she felt like performing. I did not have any special talents so often ended up being the Master of Ceremonies for such events.

In the first years after entering the convent, we could only write one letter home a week and received mail once a week. Our mail both ways could be opened and read by our 'superiors'. We were allowed only one visit a month by our families. If we were lucky, we developed a deep interior life and a stern self-discipline. Finding these medieval practices not to their liking, many of the women chose to leave during those two years. Others were sent home with little explanation, which was painful for those of us who remained and could leave a life-long scar on some who went. I never understood the secrecy surrounding these departures. Many who left stayed closely connected to each other and with us and remained good friends. They even became a lifeline and a refuge when things were tough and we needed some comfort and a home away from home.

Two incidents that happened to me in the novitiate, though minor, reveal the kind of rigid austerity that was practiced then. Sister Paul Miriam was in charge of our training. She was wise and witty but also strict. She chose the books we read. I enjoyed the writings of Cardinal Newman, St Augustine and Theresa of Avila but I disliked the story of Therese of Lisieux. She entered the Carmelite community aged fourteen and died ten years later of tuberculosis. She never ventured outside the convent walls and took pleasure in doing small penances and acts of kindness to the other sisters. 'I find it very soupy and uninspiring', I told Sr Paul when I returned it. 'Read it again', she ordered and gave it back to me. 'Even if I read it ten times, I won't change my opinion', I rashly replied. For my penance, I was told to say the rosary on my knees on the cold stone floor of the chapel. Breaking about five more rules, I snuck down to the chapel after lights out so no one would see me doing my penance. Ironically, much later in life, I would espouse the 'little way' of St Therese and preach about her during retreats to seminarians and young sisters in Kenya and Zimbabwe.

As I mentioned, we were allowed one visit a year from our families. My parents made the long drive from Pittsburgh to Massachusetts in a raging snow storm. At the end of the visit, we were expected to say our farewells in the parlor where we met. My parents had bought a new car and wanted me to see it. I accompanied them to the parking lot and admired the standard Chevy as we said our good-byes. I received another punishment for breaking the rules. I think that I told the novice mistress this rule punished our parents and should be abolished. 'I wonder why they keep you', my mother mused some years later as I continued to question and to ignore some of the more stringent rules and regulations that seemed meaningless and out of date.

Although the convent was a regimented and austere life, I appreciated the balance of work, prayer and study that we practiced in the novitiate. Sometimes it felt like we were in a summer camp or a college dorm as the sixty women who entered with me found ways to have fun and tease each other. We also found ways around many of the regulations. Our wise and experienced mentors probably knew exactly what we were up to when we snuck ice cream into the dormitories or smoked in the bathrooms, but they kept their distance and treated us as adults.

My favorite part of the novitiate in Topsfield, Massachusetts, was the visits by missioners who were home for their renewal. The talks that they gave us, full of humor and real-life drama, filled me with longing to complete these years of preparation and be on my way. Far from being on our way after we made our first vows in 1963, we were informed that we were to enter a Sister Formation Program that would mean several more years of training. Inwardly I groaned and wondered if I would persevere a further delay in realizing my dream.

5

Exposure to Mission in Practice

We returned to the Maryknoll Center at Ossining, New York, where we had started out before going to the novitiate. There we were exposed to the theology of the Second Vatican Council that had started in October of the previous year. During these next years we listened to such luminaries as Bishop Mark McGrath of Panama, Ivan Illich, the radical director of a language and cultural institute in Cuernavaca, Mexico, Bishop Dom Helder Camara of Recife, Brazil and Barry Ulanov, writer and critic. We read the liberation theologians from South America and were exposed to the anti-war activities of the Berrigan Brothers, Dan and Phil. Our minds were stretched and our ideas challenged as we unlearned much of the previous two years of rigid practice and traditional theology.

There was some confusion as we moved to a less structured life style. Instead of reciting the Divine Office five times a day, we were responsible for our own prayer and for organizing our day. We were no longer in silence and could go out overnight to visit family and friends. This was such a change that some sisters rejected it and left the community. I celebrated the changes but sometimes went overboard in embracing them. In one case, a friend and I were stranded in New York City as we had missed the last train to Ossining. We crashed on the couch of a young man that we had met in our ministry and snuck out early in the morning to catch the first train back before we would be missed. These and other reckless adventures could have been a disaster but Providence or just common sense saved me as I gradually adopted a more balanced routine.

Much later, I realized that the outward trappings of religious life were not what mattered. A genuine vocation does not depend on wearing a habit or adhering to a regimented and restrictive way of life but is implanted deep within and is tested by events. I made mistakes as I searched for my path and was saved by an internal discipline absorbed during those early years, both at home and with the sisters. Although I continued to question aspects of our way of life, often linked to the clericalism of the institutional church, I never doubted that this was where God wanted me to be.

As junior professed, we were assigned to various tasks. I could hardly believe my good fortune when sent to work in the Communications Office with Sr Maria del Rey, the Pittsburgh journalist who was largely responsible for my vocation. A free spirit, she introduced me not only to the craft of writing but also to the wisdom of our founder, Mary Josephine Rogers, who became known as Mother Mary Joseph. Sr Maria del Rey entertained me with wonderful stories that illustrated Mother's down-to-earth common sense as well as her sense of humor. 'Mother Mary Joseph would never agree to the rigid way of life we have now', she would say as she blithely broke the rules, talking after hours, keeping food in her office, taking us neophytes on joy rides in a small blue Volkswagen that was donated to us by a lay volunteer.

Sr Maria del Rey took me with her to meet the editors of the

New York Times and *Look* magazine, where she managed to get coverage for our work overseas. In those days, we had a one-hour television show on Sunday morning on NBC called *Let's Talk About God*. It was a popular puppet show for children that combined music and mission stories. We loved to go into the studio in New York for the weekly taping and made friends with all the crew. Annually, Sr Maria del Rey invited them to Maryknoll for a picnic on our spacious and beautiful grounds that included a softball game and ice cream cones. She taught me the importance of relationships and of being down to earth and true to one's self. Although she was a famous writer, to them she was a fun-loving grandmother who encouraged them to have a good time.

One publisher invited us to have dinner at Trader Vic's in New York City. As we walked into this well-known watering hole for writers, I watched every head turn to follow these two weird creatures wearing full length grey habits and black veils. Sr Maria del Rey sailed through the crowd as if she belonged there and I followed meekly in her footsteps, embarrassed to stand out as a freak. I later gained her kind of confidence as I saw how much she was appreciated and that what she wore, made no difference.

During the summers, we worked in various community programs in New York City and in Ossining, where Maryknoll was located. We were given very little instruction but dropped off on the street corner in one of the poorest sections of the community and told to go and meet people and make friends. This was the best preparation for mission that I could have had. Our wise foundress told us that we would be going to countries where we would be outsiders and not always welcome. Therefore, it would be up to us to reach out to them. We were not intended to stay in our convents praying, but to go out to the markets, the wells and the places where people gathered and start talking to them. It was essential that we learn the local language so that we could bridge the barrier between our neighbors and ourselves.

Thanks to the Second Vatican Council, we abandoned wearing the habit after 1965 and were allowed to experiment with lay clothes. The African Americans with whom I worked in Ossining were delighted. 'Honey child, I'm so glad to see that you have legs and hair on your head', exclaimed Margaret Opie, a charismatic leader who took us under her wing and made us welcome in the Black community. She fed me okra and chitlins and put me at ease in this new environment.

Joan Bloomfield, another community activist, drove us in her van to various meetings and ecumenical events. Divorced and a recovering alcoholic, Joan was passionate about AA and lobbied to have alcohol banned like drugs.

These were the days of the War Against Poverty, launched by President Johnson. A dynamic Jewish woman headed the Ossining office and welcomed the help of young Catholic sisters. We tutored, ran recreational programs for children, lobbied against slum housing, and showed films on the sides of buildings on hot summer evenings. These skills of community building and advocacy would serve me well in my next assignment overseas. I gained confidence and loved every minute of getting to know our neighbors.

In 1968 I was told that I would be going to Marquette University in Wisconsin to complete my college education. I wasn't told why I was chosen to study outside rather than at our very own Mary Rogers College, where most of my group went but I was excited by this opportunity. I joined three Maryknoll Sisters studying to be doctors at Marquette Medical School and was swept up in the anti-war and civil rights movement. The medical students taught me how to deliver babies and I introduced them to civil disobedience as we burned draft cards, marched in protest against the Vietnam War and in support of civil rights, and picketed grocery stores that sold anti-union lettuce and grapes. When we learned of the tragic death of Martin Luther King, we processed down the main street of Milwaukee singing 'We Shall Overcome' and redoubled our efforts to combat the racism rampant in the country.

I majored in theology and anthropology with a minor in mass media. It was the media studies that brought a competition for my services when I completed my degree. My heart sank when I was told that I might be sent to Hong Kong or Bolivia, where Maryknoll was active in the field of social communications. Almost in tears, I told Sr Dolores Marie Jansen, a member of the Council, my dream of being a missionary in Africa. I held my breath when the assignments were announced in the dining room a few days later. 'Janice McLaughlin – East Africa'. I rejoiced that my dream was finally coming true. It had been a long, winding road but each step of the journey had been a revelation that prepared me for the future.

6

Follow the Yellow Brick Road:
The Way to Kenya

I had a complete set of the Oz books as I was growing up. Reading of Dorothy's adventures in this magical kingdom, I was mesmerized by her quest to meet the Wizard of Oz. On the way, she meets the cowardly lion, the tin woodman and the scarecrow, each of them seeking a gift from the kindly wizard in the Emerald City. 'Follow, follow the Yellow Brick Road', they sing as they make the journey together, overcoming various obstacles along the way.

My journey to East Africa, in 1969, was not unlike Dorothy's journey in Oz, a new country, full of strange and magical creatures. Like her companions, I was also seeking certain gifts that would enable me to be a heroic missioner, who would face martyrdom with courage. I had read the lives of the saints and was convinced that to be a martyr was the highest possible calling. I was inspired by the stories of Maryknoll martyrs Sister Agneta Chang, who was killed during the Korean War, Bishop Francis Ford who died in China and Bishop Patrick Byrne who suffered and died on a long march in the freezing cold winter of North Korea. Little could I imagine that Maryknoll would have more martyrs within the next eleven years and that one of them would be Ita Ford with whom I entered.

I left New York with great expectations and unstoppable excitement. My studies in mass media made me 'marketable' and I had been offered places in Malawi, Tanzania and Kenya. Maryknoll Father Joseph Healey, a fellow journalist, arranged for me to visit various communication centers on my way to the Maryknoll language school in Musoma, Tanzania. My intrepid and fun-loving travelling companions, Sisters Anita Magovern and Bernice Rigney, found bargain accommodation, listed in our copy of *Europe on Five Dollars a Day,* as we stopped in Dublin, London, Paris, Rome, Addis Ababa and Nairobi. Anita and Bern went sightseeing each day while I dutifully visited media training centers at each stop.

I still marvel that experienced church personnel took time from their busy schedules to explain their media ministry to a 25-year-old newcomer, fresh out of college, with an Afro hairdo and wearing a mini-skirt. Later I sent Kenyans to study journalism and broadcasting at the training centers I had visited in Dublin and London and some of these graduates would contribute to Vatican Radio. This international exposure was an auspicious beginning to my mission career and cemented a life-long friendship with Fr Healey, who made it possible.

I was filled with excitement on the last leg of the journey, a flight over Lake Victoria on a small plane that went from Entebbe, Uganda, to Musoma, Tanzania. We experienced a terrific thunderstorm as we flew over the huge lake. As the plane bounced and rolled, I was certain that I would never reach my destination but would drown in the lake. When land finally came into sight and the plane started to descend, I relaxed and thanked all my ancestors and angels and saints who had spared us and allowed my dream of living and working on this continent to come true.

The arrival in Musoma was an indication of what was to come. The dirt runway was a resting place for cows and goats which had to be chased away to allow the plane to land. The children in the nearby village watched as these strangers touched down. As we came down the rickety stairs of the plane, the children swarmed around wanting to touch our skin and hair. '*Mzungu, Mzungu,*' (white person, white person) they shouted as they took our hands and led us to the Sisters waiting to welcome us to our new home.

The Maryknoll Language School at Musoma on Lake Victoria, Tanzania, was about as far as you could get from the ancient historical attractions of London, Paris and Rome where we had just been. Beautifully situated on the shores of the lake, it was home to many varieties of snakes, colonies of safari ants and every kind of insect imaginable. The mosquito net over my bed also became a source of amusement to my travelling companions. Bern and Anita killed themselves laughing when I would go screaming out of the house each time a rubber snake they put there, dropped out of the net onto my bed. I never stopped falling for this practical joke, which helped to relieve the intensity of the language study.

Another stress breaker was the Saturday night movies that were shown at the nearby Family Life Center run by Maryknollers Dave Jones and Margaret Monroe and a Tanzanian lay couple. A packed hall of local families gathered for these weekly events that usually featured Charlie Chaplin or Laurel and Hardy. These slap-stick silent films had us join the people rolling in the aisles laughing. Such simple pleasures prepared us for making our own fun in remote places where there was no other entertainment and the nights were long and dark, without electricity, TV or computers.

We spent our days learning Swahili words and in the evenings, we were in the language lab listening to tapes to help our pronunciation. The curriculum included lectures on Tanzania history and culture by historians, anthropologists, economists and political scientists. Sr Anita McWilliam, the Maryknoll linguist who ran the school with Maryknoll priest Phil Sheerin, introduced us to the grammar and taught us how to interact with our Tanzania neighbors.

In 1967, President Julius Nyerere issued the Arusha Declaration, a statement of the tenets of Tanzanian socialism, a dominant theme of which was *ujamaa,* 'extended family' or 'brotherhood'. *Ujamaa* asserts that 'a person becomes a person *through the people* or community. The spirit of ‹others› or ‹community› brings units of families together and fosters cohesion, love, and service'. We became ardent proponents of this philosophy of familyhood that underpinned the politics of this independent nation, trying to chart its own course and proposing an African type of socialism in keeping with the continent's culture and values.

After four months of study and a month practicing my language skills, I was prepared to embark on my first mission assignment as Communications Secretary for the Catholic Bishops' Conference of Kenya. Eager for my next adventure, I boarded the lake steamer in Musoma for an overnight journey to Kisumu, Kenya, where I caught a train to my new home in Nairobi. Along the yellow brick road of my journey, I had acquired some of the gifts that I would need – the courage of the lion, a kindly heart like the tin woodman and the inquisitive mind that the scarecrow craved as well as the gift of laughing at the hardships, foibles and failures that inevitably come when living in another culture. Unlike Dorothy and her dog Toto, I had no desire to return to my safe and familiar home in the United States.

7

Karibuni: Kenyan Hospitality

In 1970, the East Africa Community that had been formed in 1967 to build ties between Tanzania, Kenya and Uganda on Lake Victoria, was still operating and the lake steamer was one of the practical signs of this harmony. There was a common currency in the EAC and a common postal service.

I slept on a chair on the deck with the cool breeze from the lake blowing the mosquitos away. We arrived in Kisumu, the heart of the Luo people of western Kenya, in the morning. The train ride to Nairobi was through the lush green highlands, tea estates of Kericho and the wide plains of the Rift Valley where giraffe, leopards and antelopes roamed. It was like the Garden of Eden. I was among the first Maryknoll Sisters to work in Kenya. Sr Marion Puscz, a doctor, worked in the government hospital in Machakos and Sisters Paula Kunz and Noel Doescher, who were nurses, worked in the government hospital in Malindi. Soon more Maryknoll Sisters would arrive to staff a new Catholic hospital in Kinango outside of Mombasa on the coast.

The Maryknoll Fathers welcomed me to Nairobi and settled me in a room at Flora Hostel, a boarding house for working women in Nairobi that was run by Consolata Sisters from Italy. It was a good place as it put me in touch with young Kenyan women who told me about their lives and their hopes for the future. It was also a meeting place for missionaries from all over the country who stayed there when they came to Nairobi for medical appointments, purchasing supplies and for a retreat and vacation.

A few months after my arrival, two other Maryknoll Sisters came to Nairobi from Tanzania to join me. Mary Bowes was a nurse and one of the first Maryknoll Sisters to come to East Africa. She helped to set up and train the Immaculate Heart Sisters (IHM)), a local Tanzanian community that is well known and respected. When they elected their first superior, Mary decided it was time to move on. With her wealth of experience and medical background, she was offered a job with Catholic Relief Services in Kenya. Edith Fragola had taken a course at Cody Institute in Nova Scotia in cooperative management that she was implementing with women's groups in Tanzania. Edie was a gourmet cook and full of fun. With the Christian Council of Kenya, she set up a project for the disabled in Mathare Valley, the biggest slum in Nairobi at the time.

'Let's move to our own place', Edie suggested after a few months in Flora Hostel. We found a two-story flat on the outskirts of Nairobi that was owned by a Kenyan businessman. Edie, Mary and I didn't know each other when we moved into Jamhuri Estate and we spent long hours each day talking about our work and about our impressions of Kenya. I was much younger than either of them and had not yet made my final commitment or vows in the Maryknoll congregation. I often came home late and forgot to do my household chores, but I never felt judged or scolded. Edie and Mary would simply remind me and encourage me. 'The bathroom floor could use a scrub', they might say, or, 'Can we show you how to cook pasta'? 'What time will you be back'? With their understanding and support, I learned the importance of being transparent and not hiding my whereabouts. 'Tonight, I may be back about midnight', I told them and invited them to join my students and me for a graduation celebration at Starlight nightclub. They declined the offer and did not complain when I came home late, excited by my first time ever to dance at a nightclub, still dizzy from the strobe lights and humming the tunes of a live band.

I listened and learned, excited to be in the capital city of a country that I had studied about in high school. In fact, I had written my history term paper on the Mau Mau uprising in Kenya, which had taken the lives of many Kenyans who were fighting for freedom from British rule. Jomo Kenyatta, who had been imprisoned, was seen to be their leader. I had read Kenyatta's book, *Facing Mount Kenya*, which describes many aspects of Kikuyu culture. I also read a book by the head of the British forces who wrote of the capture and death of Dedan Kimathi, the leader of the guerrilla forces. Years later, a play about Kimathi in which I was involved, would link Kenya and Zimbabwe. The Kenya Catholic Secretariat, where I had my office, was located in the center of Nairobi in an office building on the corner of Kenyatta Avenue and Muindi Mbingu Street. The main market was a few blocks away as was the University of Nairobi and the broadcast house for the Voice of Kenya. I couldn't ask for a better location.

Not long after my arrival, I walked the few blocks to the University of Nairobi to meet with the head of the Literature Department, Mr Jimmy Stewart. Jimmy was an exile from South Africa, a devout Catholic and a communist. He introduced me to some of the other members of staff – leading lights on the African literary scene like Taban lo Liyong, Okot p'bitek, Ngugi wa Thiongo and Michere Mugo. I had started my introduction to East Africa by reading the African Writers' Series put out by Heinemann Books so these names were not new to me. I won friends easily by praising their work and asking questions about it. Eventually most of them would participate in writer's workshops that I helped to organize for youth.

Jimmy also put me in touch with prominent Catholics in the country who I recruited to do radio and TV broadcasts. At that time in Kenya, the churches were given many hours of free airtime. Each day began and ended on the Voice of Kenya with a prayer and a reflection or sermon by a member of one of the many Christian churches. One of my tasks was to recruit the Catholics and to train them how to write and deliver a script.

Training thus became the main focus of my work. With the support of Fr Joe Healey, I recruited a Kenyan who would work with me and eventually replace me. This was our missionary aim – to work ourselves out of a job and move on to more needy places. John Irungu had just graduated from a Catholic high school in Nairobi. In response to the advertisement that I had placed in the Catholic newspaper, he submitted some of his writing. I was intrigued and invited him for an interview. With his winning smile and positive personality, John was selected as my local counterpart. We worked well as a team with his interest in broadcasting and mine in journalism.

One of our first successes was a three-week course in mass media that we ran for leaders in the church – priests, sisters and laity. From this pool of talent, we recruited our broadcasters for 'Voice of Kenya' and our diocesan communication teams. Later we ran courses for the Catholic bishops in which some of Kenya's top broadcasters agreed to serve as trainers. The bishops enthusiastically volunteered to do mock interviews with people like VOK's Norbert Okare, who was as well known in Kenya as anchor-man Walter Cronkite was in the United States. After this training, the bishops were no longer shy about issuing statements and giving interviews to the media.

Another coup in those early days was the arrival of Fr Michael Traber, SMB, who had been deported from what was then Rhodesia. Fr Traber, the publisher of *Moto*, a monthly periodical that commented on current affairs, was deported for a cartoon that showed Africans being crushed by White hands dripping with blood. The caption, quoted a government White Paper: 'The proposed new Constitution will ensure that government will remain in responsible hands.'

I set up press conferences for Fr Traber who was interviewed extensively by the Kenyan press, radio and television, giving a first-hand account of the situation in White-ruled Rhodesia. I would later receive phone calls, asking me if I had another Michael Traber for them to interview! That cemented my reputation and gave me credibility within the media community.

Mike became a good friend and introduced me to the liberation struggle in Zimbabwe. He knew many of the leaders, who had come from Catholic schools, and told me of the work of the Catholic Commission for Justice and Peace (CCJP). After that I wrote reviews for the Kenyan papers of the publications by CCJP and I also drafted statements for the Kenyan Bishops' Conference in support of majority rule in Rhodesia.

Most exciting for me were the ecumenical contacts that I was making at that time. I grew up before Vatican II when relationships between Catholics and Protestants were not encouraged. I could not, for example, join the Girl Scouts because they met in the basement of a local Protestant Church nor could my family attend the wedding of a friend in a Presbyterian Church. We took those restrictions very seriously and knew that if a Catholic married a Protestant, he or she would have to pledge in writing to have the children raised as Catholics. I went to the local Catholic school and most of my friends and all my relatives on both sides of the family were Catholic. This very homogenous background and the Maryknoll training I had received did little to prepare me for the diverse world I would encounter in Kenya.

It was a new and liberating experience to be working with Protestants of various denominations from various countries. I collaborated with the Christian Council of Kenya (NCCK) not only in the media work but also in organizing demonstrations in support of freedom for the people of Angola, Mozambique, Namibia, Rhodesia and South Africa. As I was the only Maryknoll Sister in Nairobi for some time, my Protestant counterparts took me under their wing and invited me to their homes and to their services. A group of us from the Christian Council, All Africa Council of Churches and the Catholic Secretariat, formed a prayer group that met monthly to reflect on current affairs in the light of scripture. We came from Liberia, Cameroon, Uganda, Kenya, Ireland and USA. Even though I had studied scripture in the novitiate, I learned how deficient I was in comparison to my Protestant counterparts who practically knew the Bible by heart and could easily quote chapter and verse. The sharing was deep and personal and quite a change from reciting the Divine Office or saying a few responses at Mass. It was liberating for me to realize that God's Word in Scripture was alive and spoke to my daily life.

I was also a member of a study group that met to discuss books such as Walter Rodney's *How Europe Underdeveloped Africa* and Colin Leys classic, *Underdevelopment in Kenya – The Political Economy of Neo-Colonialism, 1964-1971.* I was getting a crash course in radical politics and mixing with a wide range of Kenyans and international church personnel. I taught journalism classes at the All Africa Conference of Churches Communication Training Center and was a member of the board. This put me in touch with well-known figures such as Canon Burgess Carr, the Secretary General of the AACC who was from Liberia, Kenneth Best, another Liberian who headed the media division and Canon Yinka Olumide, Director of the AACC Training Center, who came from Nigeria.

They were outspoken in their views about colonialism and the neo-colonialism which was engulfing countries that had gained their political freedom but were still in economic bondage to outside forces. The churches were not exempt from this critique. Canon Carr issued a moratorium on missionaries coming from the industrial countries to the North, arguing that they brought with them the baggage of capitalist ideology and racist superiority. His call for a halt to the mission enterprise brought much soul-searching and discussion, especially in the World Council of Churches that had close ties to the AACC.

I wondered if I was included in this critique? I was aware that I had come with certain assumptions and a romanticized view of all things African but I was becoming critical of some aspects of the culture, especially its treatment of women. Domestic violence was common as was polygamy. Few of my staff or women friends knew how much their husbands earned and had to beg each month for money for basic household expenses. While I viewed this arrangement as oppressive, I did not attempt to introduce 'women's liberation' or feminism into my work but did advocate for the end of apartheid in South Africa and minority rule in Southern Rhodesia. I assumed that I didn't fit the description of the 'ugly American' implied by the moratorium.

In addition to my work at the Catholic Secretariat I also taught media studies at the AACC Training Center to students from a variety of African countries including Ethiopia, Swaziland, Ghana, Nigeria, Cameroon, Tanzania and Kenya. On one of my trips back to the States, I took advantage of the Pan-American Airlines offer of unlimited stops free of charge to visit former students in Ethiopia, Ghana, Cameroon, and Nigeria. I marveled at the diversity of this huge continent and began to understand that one could not generalize about 'Africa'.

My first return trip to the States was in 1974. During this renewal period of three months, I gained a deeper understanding of foreign affairs and the importance of advocacy. Sr Annette Mulry, who headed our Office of Global Concerns, involved me and two other sisters with mission experience in East Africa to draft a statement against the appointment of Nathanial Davis as Secretary of State for African Affairs. He had been an Ambassador in Guatemala when the US government had interfered there and it was feared that he would do the same in southern Africa. Although I was the youngest and least experienced, they chose me to deliver the statement before the Senate Foreign Relations Commission since I had recently come from the African continent and would soon return. Although my knees were shaking, I delivered the statement clearly and with confidence. This was the first of several appearances before congressional committees over the years. It taught me the importance of citizen participation and the need for thorough research and preparation as well as partnership with others. In this case, we had joined the American Committee on Africa (ACOA) to voice our objections. Although Davis was appointed, he later opposed the intervention of the CIA in Angola and Namibia and retired from the State Department.

I returned to Kenya with a deeper understanding and appreciation of the US system of governance that gave citizens an opportunity to voice their views. Jomo Kenyatta was President of Kenya at this time and was an imposing figure who had been detained, as we saw, during the liberation struggle as the leader of the nationalists. Although Nairobi was a very cosmopolitan city that served as a media hub for many international news outlets, there was unrest in the west of the country. Tom Mboya, an outstanding leader in the Luo community, had been shot and killed in the streets of Nairobi and Oginga Odinga, former Vice President, was detained when I was newly arrived in Kenya. There were suspicions about auto accidents that took the lives of other leaders such as Ronald Ngala and Pio Pinto. One could feel the tension beneath the surface and the simmering resentment against the Kikuyu who were seen to be monopolizing power and resources, such as land.

At that time, the Kenya Episcopal Conference was small, consisting of six dioceses and two prefectures. Cardinal Maurice Otunga was the leader of the Church in Kenya. He came from the West of the country and was proud to say that he was the son of a chief who had 20 wives. He was a kind and gentle person and very traditional in his views of church and state. However, the bishops spoke out to condemn a resumption of oath-taking among the Kikuyu, harking back to the Mau Mau experience. Their statement was widely covered by the media and seemed to have put a stop to this development. This gave the hierarchy confidence that their voice was heard and respected and they asked me to draft various statements for them that supported liberation in southern Africa, opposed the concordat between the Portuguese government and the church in Mozambique, criticized the civil war in Sudan and commented on local issues as well. My communications office began to double as a Justice and peace outlet and local and international media were knocking at our door.

My parents came to visit me during my second year in Kenya. I showed them the beautiful sights that draw tourists to Kenya – Treetops Lodge in the Aberdare Mountains where we viewed elephants and buffalo from the safety of our balcony; Amboseli Game Park where we watched herds of animals waiting their turn to drink at the watering hole at the base of the cliff below the lodge; and Mombasa, where we swam in the warm water of the Indian Ocean and toured Fort Jesus, the site of the early Portuguese explorers who followed the coast of Africa in the wake of Vasco de Gama.

I also introduced my parents to my work and to my friends. We visited rural homes where there was no indoor plumbing, electricity or running water. On their final day we visited a poor urban community on the outskirts of Nairobi. When my mother saw the plastic and cardboard dwellings and the miserable surroundings, she broke down in tears. 'I can't possibly go inside,' she told me between sobs. 'It is too heartbreaking to see that people live like this.' My father and I entered the simple home and ate the refreshments we were served, explaining that my mother wasn't feeling well. When we left, the family came to the car and presented my mother with a basket that the women had made.

That evening, before going to the airport, we took the other Maryknoll Sisters in Nairobi out to eat at a local restaurant. Tears streamed down my mother's face throughout the meal and she hardly touched the food. The sisters thought she was sad to be leaving me behind but my father and I knew that she was crying out of sorrow for the poverty she had witnessed as well as the kindness of these destitute people who shared the little they had with us. This is the deeper story of mission and I was happy that my parents had experienced it, even though it was painful.

After two years in Kenya, it was time for me to make a decision about whether I would continue as a Maryknoll Sister. I was happy in my work and in my community living but I struggled with making vows of poverty, chastity and obedience for the rest of my life. 'I can't say yes forever, but only for one day at a time.' With this understanding I agreed to make my final commitment and chose to have a small simple ceremony with our sisters in Kitale, in the west of Kenya. We could add our own words to the universal vow formula at that time of experimentation. Paraphrasing something that Paulo Freire had written, I vowed that I would commit myself to the quest for justice and would strive to create a more human and loving world. This celebration helped me to remain in Maryknoll but did not resolve my doubts and my misgivings that would surface from time to time, especially when I felt caged in by rules and by an institutional model of church and religious life. Yet I persisted in my vocation. Was it out of stubbornness? Was it a superstitious belief that I would be punished if I turned my back on this calling or was it a genuine desire to follow Christ; 'to act justly, to love tenderly and to walk humbly with God' (Micah 6.8)?

I thrived in the work that I was doing and made many friends. I could have happily remained in Kenya for as long as I stayed healthy but God had other plans. They were revealed to me on my birthday of that year – 13 February, 1977, when our good friends Anne Hope and Sally Timmel, renowned for putting Paulo Freire's philosophy of adult education into practice, invited me and my housemates, Sisters Edith Fragola and Mary Bowes, to their house for supper. At the end of the meal, Anne showed me a letter that she had received from the Catholic Institute for International Relations (CIIR) in London inviting her to go to Rhodesia to serve as the Press Secretary for the Catholic Commission for Justice and Peace (CCJP). The request was to start a newsletter and to train a local Zimbabwean to take over within a year.

Handing me the letter, Anne asked, 'Wouldn't you like to do this?' Without a moment's hesitation, I said yes. I knew immediately that this was meant for me. I am the kind of person who can take days to make a simple decision like what pair of shoes to buy or blouse to wear but I have no difficulty in making life-changing decisions such as this. Full of excitement, I took the letter to the bishop chairperson of the Communications Department and asked if I could go. Everything fell into place almost miraculously.

The bishops said yes and a young Kenyan who had just returned from journalism studies agreed to take my place at the Catholic Secretariat for a year. I was on my way by the end of May, just three months after I received the unexpected invitation that would change my life.

8

On the Frontline in War-Torn Rhodesia

My arrival in Salisbury, Rhodesia, was like a comedy gone awry. My connection through Lusaka, Zambia, was delayed so I arrived in the evening instead of the afternoon as scheduled. I had no way to communicate with Brother Arthur, the Organizing Secretary of CCJP, the Catholic Commission for Justice and Peace, so there was no one to meet me at the airport and I had no Rhodesian money. I explained my predicament to the driver of the airport bus who kindly took me into the center of the city and called a taxi driver friend who took me to a nearby hotel to spend the night. I marveled that these African men were so helpful and kind when I knew there was a war going on that pitted the white rulers against the majority of black citizens. No one talked about the war and the city seemed very calm, clean and modern.

When I called the CCJP office in the morning, Brother Arthur was shocked to learn that I had arrived since he had presumed, I would come the next day. He was even more shocked to learn where I had spent the night at the Queen's Hotel which had a reputation for drinking and prostitution. I assured him I had a

46

peaceful night and there were no midnight knocks on the door. I was often teased about my dramatic arrival and my choice of resting place. I will always remember the bus and taxi drivers who came to my rescue and the hotel that gave me a room even though I couldn't pay them. It was a good beginning and taught me not to fall for stereotypes about black and white but to trust the goodness of people and accept their help when it is offered.

The CCJP Committee met me for supper a few days later at a more proper hotel. I remember thinking how much they enjoyed each other's company and how much fun we were having, even though a war was being fought in the rural areas. I learned how they supported each other and kept their spirits up with prayer and friendship. The Bible passage, 'See how these Christians love one another', suited this group to a tee – even though they weren't all Christian.

I was taken to stay at St Anne's Hospital which was run by the Little Company of Mary, popularly known as the Blue Nuns because of the color of their habits. The Sisters were very kind and welcoming. I soon learned that there was a big difference between the sisters who staffed this urban hospital where most of the patients were white and some had fought in the war against the guerrilla forces and their fellow 'blue' sisters who worked at rural mission hospitals where they came into contact with the guerrillas and saw the atrocities carried out by soldiers of Ian Smith's Rhodesian forces .These Sisters on the frontline of the struggle could not speak of this to their own Sisters in town who might withdraw them from what were seen as dangerous war zones. But they brought their stories to the Justice and Peace Commission where I worked. We sometimes stayed up late at night talking in the convent as they felt free to share their experiences with me and were happy to be serving the needy in the rural areas even though it was risky and dangerous .I was mesmerized by their tales and had a great respect for their courage and commitment.

The Justice and Peace Office was located in an old house across the street from the Dominican Convent School in downtown Harare. The Catholic Social Services and Development office (CSSD) was in the house next to it and its director, Sr Dymphna Van Wesenbeeck, a Sister of Charity from Holland, became a good friend. She lived in an apartment with Marta, her sister-in-law from Angola, and Nella, Marta's daughter. They were learning English before they would go to Holland to live with Dymphna's brother. In the evenings when Dymphna invited me to dine with them, Nella and I would dance to the music of *Ibi Tombi* while Dymphna and Marta prepared the meal. On weekends, Jesuit Fr Ted Rogers, Director of the School of Social Work, sometimes took the four of us on picnics to nearby Lake Chivero where we played ball on the lawn overlooking the lake and enjoyed a simple lunch of cheese, fruit and bread. The war seemed far away during relaxing times like these.

Opposite our office were several tall office blocks that housed some of the Rhodesian government offices. Brother Arthur assumed that they spied on our office, taking photos of anyone who entered .He was a master of intrigue and developed codes for talking on the phone with the assumption that the phones and offices were bugged. Each month a technician came to de-bug the offices but they soon were under surveillance again, such was the level of mistrust that existed at that time between the Catholic Church and the Rhodesian government headed by Ian Douglas Smith.

In February 1977, four Dominican nuns and two Jesuit priests and a brother had been killed at Musami, a Catholic mission just an hour from Harare. The government blamed the guerrillas, whom they called terrorists, for this atrocity while the Church suspected a shady government force called the Selous Scouts that impersonated guerrillas and carried out horrible acts in order to discredit the genuine freedom fighters .One of my tasks was to investigate this incident.

Bishop Donal Lamont, a fiery Irish orator and chair of CCJP, had become a thorn in the side of the government, with his strong rejection of its policies and its conduct of the war. I had admired him from afar when I read his statements and reviewed the reports put out by the Commission that he headed. He had been deported before I arrived but I had met him in March when I came to Salisbury to be interviewed for the post. He was then under house arrest at St Anne's Hospital and used to joke that if others found out about this comfortable arrangement, they would be competing to be under house arrest. On St Patrick's Day, he played the piano and recited Irish poems. He also invited one of the older sisters to dance with him, much to her embarrassment. Although I didn't spend much time with him, I let him know how much I admired his stand and that I had written about it, when I wa in Kenya. I remained in touch with him throughout the years and we met in Ireland many years later where he showed me his prize possessions – a complete set of the works of John Cardinal Newman and a citation that he had been awarded by Pope John Paul II for his stand against injustice in Rhodesia. 'I had to follow my conscience', he told me, 'Even though it meant that I was not in agreement with the other bishops'.

On my first morning on the job, Brother Arthur introduced me to Dr Luisa Guidotti, a member of an Italian lay missionary organization who worked at All Soul's Mission Hospital in Mutoko, 150 km north east of Salisbury (Harare). The area was a highly contested war zone not far from the border with Mozambique. Luisa told me of attending all night meetings, *pungwes*, where the guerrillas would teach the people the reason why they were fighting, listing the injustices of the white settler government.

They also sang freedom songs that were adapted from Christian hymns. Luisa made it sound very positive and uplifting. She told me of the time that the guerrillas shelled the mission hospital and the patients had to hide under the beds. 'It's a good thing they had such poor aim', she said with a chuckle. No one was hurt and the buildings were not damaged. She told me that the guerrilla commander came to apologize a few days later. 'They had made a mistake', he told her contritely.

Luisa was warm, joyful and outgoing. She made no distinctions in her medical service and treated anyone who came for help. She realized that some of the patients were most likely guerrillas or their supporters. She served all with love and gentle care. In 1979, Rhodesian forces shot her in the hip as she drove down the road to the hospital in a well-marked mission ambulance and she bled to death before she could get help. Her death affected me deeply. Although I had only met her a few times, I viewed Luisa as the ideal missionary, full of joy and obviously in love with the people she served.

Sister Rocha Mushonga, superior of the diocesan religious community, the Little Children of Our Blessed Lady (LCBL), was another of my early teachers about the war. She came to our offices to report that one of their sisters had been arrested at a rural mission. I took copious notes as she told me the story of Sr Irene Rufaro, a nurse at Mount St Mary's Mission who was accused by the Rhodesian police of supporting the guerrillas. She was taken to the police camp at the nearby town of Wedza, denied food and was not allowed to wear her veil or religious dress. Repeatedly the police questioned her about a letter they had found in her possession from a young man in the area who they suspected was a local guerrilla commander. We helped Mother Rocha get a lawyer and Irene was released after almost a month in detention .I wrote up my notes and submitted a report to the Bishops Conference.

Irene, Rocha and I would have many more fateful encounters before the war was over.

Another case in which I was involved was that of Ranga Zinyemba, student leader at the University of Southern Rhodesia. He found out that his office had been searched and that the Special Branch had found incriminating letters indicating that he was helping students to leave the country to join the guerrilla forces. By then, he was under restriction, which meant that he could not leave the township where he stayed. Fearing for his safety, Brother Arthur sent me to the Air Zimbabwe office to buy a ticket for Ranga to travel from Bulawayo to Johannesburg. I remember sweating as I purchased the ticket, certain that the clerk at the airline office knew what I was doing and that the police would swoop down and arrest me for assisting a supporter of 'terrorism'.

Before he left the country, Ranga wished to marry Alice. The simple wedding ceremony took place the evening of his departure. Brother Arthur, Fr Dieter Scholz, our chairperson, and I travelled to a home in an African township where Fr Scholz conducted the marriage by candlelight while Arthur and I stood by as witnesses. In those days, it was illegal for whites to be in a black township and we could only hope that the police didn't spot us. We drove away with Ranga in the car, depositing him at the main bus terminal for his journey to Bulawayo where he would board a plane to South Africa and then on to Sheffield, England, where he would study for the next few years. He would not be reunited with his wife Alice for another year.

Being involved in such clandestine activities was second nature to those who worked with the Justice and Peace Commission. They lived in daily proximity to danger and often broke the laws of white ruled Rhodesia. At this time, some of the racial barriers began to be relaxed as Ian Smith and his Rhodesian Front government bowed to international pressure and to the increasing cost of the war both in money and in lives lost. Every white Rhodesian male was 'called up' to serve in the army for at least four months each year. This was disrupting civilian industries and also exposing the white population to the obvious reality that this was a war that would not be won by a minority population whatever advantage it might have in technology and fire power.

The Smith government therefore proposed an internal settlement, bringing on board three African leaders who agreed to serve with him: Chief Chirau, who represented traditional leaders, Ndabaningi Sithole, the previous head of ZANU who had been replaced by Robert Mugabe, and Bishop Abel Muzorewa of the United Methodist Church who was president of the African National Congress, an organisation set up to oppose the British proposals in 1972 to end the impasse in Rhodesia .

Hotels and restaurants in the capital city, Salisbury, were now permitted to serve Africans. One evening I went with some African friends to the coffee shop at the Jameson Hotel to put this new ruling to a test. All heads turned as we entered and seated ourselves at a table in the center of the dining room. The waiters, who were all African, took our orders and enjoyed serving us but there were hostile stares from some of the white patrons who didn't appreciate our presence. The majority ignored us and we enjoyed our little outing. We decided to take this test the next step in the African part of town where I entered a cinema with my African friends .Again, heads turned as I, the only white person, entered the lobby. Instead of hostile stares, there was clapping and much hand shaking as I was warmly welcomed. I have no idea what film we watched, I was so overcome by this show of acceptance and friendship.

Back at the office, I continued to learn more about the war from a host of visitors who came from rural missions where they faced life and death choices each day. For instance, Franciscan Fr Pascal

Slevin, the parish priest at Mount St Mary's Mission, Wedza, about two hours SE of Salisbury, Sr Theresa Corby, a 'blue' sister and the mission doctor and Brother Juniper, also a Franciscan, brought us photographs of men who had been tortured near the mission by the Rhodesian forces. They told us stories of the brutality of the government troops against civilians who were accused of supporting the guerrillas. They also told us delightful stories of entertaining the guerrillas in the priest's sitting room .It was very clear where their sympathies lay.

When they invited me to spend a weekend at Mount St Mary's, I readily accepted, eager to get a taste of life in a war zone and hoping to meet in person the guerrillas who I had heard so much about, both positive and negative. As we drove down the rural dirt roads to reach the mission, I was aware that they could be mined and we could be blown up at any time. This was a common danger throughout the country. Being ambushed by the guerrillas was another common danger. They might 'shoot first and ask questions later'. I knew that Catholic Bishop, Adolph Schmitt, of Bulawayo, had been shot and killed on the road by guerrilla forces in 1976 while the nun who was travelling with him was spared as a witness and a warning to others.

I had never lived in a war zone and didn't know how real the danger was or how much was exaggerated. The weekend at Mount St Mary's was enjoyable but quiet. Neither the guerrillas nor the Rhodesian forces showed up. I returned to Harare a little wiser in the ways of rural mission life but I hadn't seen any real action. Little did I guess that this visit would lead to my arrest and detention.

9

The Best Retreat:
Imprisonment and Deportation

My arrival in Rhodesia in mid-1977 coincided with one of the most active years since of the war which had begun in earnest in 1972. Four Dominican nuns, two priests and a brother had been shot and killed at St Paul's Musami mission, not far from Harare in February 1977. I joined others on the Commission investigating this gruesome crime. The government immediately blamed the massacre on the 'terrorists' while many church personnel suspected that the Selous Scouts, a shadowy government force that impersonated the guerrillas, had been responsible. I was now witnessing history as it unfolded before my eyes. It was exhilarating and also frightening.

I had moved from St Anne's Hospital to a bedsitter apartment a few weeks after my arrival in order to be within walking distance of the office. This later proved to be a big mistake. Brother Arthur had given me a short-wave radio so that I could listen to the international news at night, which was a further mistake. Being trusted with sensitive information and interviewing witnesses filled my days while in the evenings I listened to the news and wrote in my diary. Fr Mike Traber, whom I had welcomed to Kenya, had encouraged me to keep a record of things as they happened since events moved so quickly. He also told me to find a good hiding place for it. He had kept his journal in a file in his office labelled 'sermon notes'. A one-room bedsitter did not offer many hiding places and I soon forgot his wise advice. This was also a big mistake.

While the fighting on the ground intensified, so did the diplomatic efforts to find a political settlement. In July we learned that representatives of the British and American governments would arrive in August to push the Anglo-American proposals, the latest peace initiative of Henry Kissinger. At our weekly planning meeting, we in the CCJP decided we needed to brief this team about the real situation on the ground. We would prepare a series of 'fact papers' about the war, in order to balance the government propaganda. My role was to write the papers.

Thrilled to be given this responsibility, I immediately started to do research into the critical subjects that the Commission deemed important. These included secret hangings, torture, propaganda, 'protected' villages, repressive legislation, and the mass murder of civilians.

Geoff Feltoe, a lawyer on the Commission, helped me draft a paper on legislation. The photos and information that we had received from Mount St Mary's Mission were used in a chapter on torture and ill treatment of civilians. That chapter included the story and photos of a young man who walked into our office one day to tell us about the beating he had received from Rhodesian soldiers. He sat perfectly straight and showed no sign of pain as he recounted his ordeal. I then took him to see Bester Kanyama, a photographer in Highfields Township who assisted us. When we arrived at his studio the young man took off his shirt and pulled down his trousers. His entire back and buttocks were covered with open wounds still oozing blood and pus. I marveled at his stoicism throughout the interview and the drive to the township. When I commented on this, he merely smiled and told me he just wanted people to know what was happening to ordinary people like him. His determination to tell the story helped him to overcome the pain.

Another chapter in the document that I was compiling for the Commission was on secret hangings. At that time, the Rhodesian government was sentencing guerrillas it had captured to death by hanging without notifying their families or giving them legal counsel. Fr Emmanuel Ribeiro, prison chaplain during much of the war, was present at each hanging to give the last rites and to pray with the accused. After each hanging, he would come to our office, looking pale and distraught, to give us vital information about each victim; information that was hidden from their families and from the public. I wrote what we knew at the time without revealing the source.

When I finished writing each paper, it went to a team of the Commission for correcting and to our lawyer to make sure that we were not breaking the law. Then the papers were sent to two overseas addresses: one to our partner in London, the Catholic Institute for International Relations (CIIR), and the other to Malcolm Smart, who worked with Amnesty International. Amazingly, all the papers reached their destination. This would soon prove to be a stroke of good luck.

I had entered the country on a temporary permit. When it was about to expire, I was told that it would not be renewed and was given a few weeks to wind up and leave the country. CCJP intended to appeal this decision and I was hopeful that I could stay the year as promised. I had completed the fact papers and we were making plans to meet with the Anglo-American delegation that would arrive in a few days.

The day before their arrival, a van pulled up in the yard and several police from the Special Branch entered our office. It was clear that they had been tipped off since they were looking for 'fact papers' about the war. They questioned Brother Arthur and then came to my office and started going through the papers on my desk. Then they started going through the filing cabinets where we kept most of our data. Excited by what they were reading, they decided to take away both filing cabinets and every paper on my desk.

When they left, Arthur called the members of the Commission and set up an emergency meeting at our offices that evening. Everyone turned up to be briefed on what had happened: Fr Dieter Scholz SJ, Mr John Deary, chairperson, Brother Fidelis Mukonori SJ, Mr Geoff Feltoe, Mrs Mary Rooney, Mr Ismael Muvingi, Mr Moses Ayema and others who I can't recall. As we recounted the search by the police, a loud banging at the back door interrupted us. Brother Arthur went to see who was there. 'We've come for Sister McLaughlin', announced one of the men from the Special Branch. Arthur stalled them at the back door while John Deary went into Arthur's office and called our lawyer, Nick McNally, to tell him what was happening. 'Don't say anything until the lawyer arrives', John cautioned me. Those were the last words I heard as I was whisked into a car and taken to my flat. I assumed that I was being deported since my appeal for an extension of my residence permit had been rejected. I don't remember feeling afraid but only disappointed that I would be leaving before I completed the work that I had been sent to do.

Two men and a woman from the police or Special Branch accompanied me into the one room where I lived and began to go through the books on the shelf. I sat on the bed while they searched and saw them take away a few of the books with a political theme. A minute too late, I saw my diary sitting in plain view on the only easy chair in the room. Before I could move to sit on it, one of the policemen picked it up, opened it at random and started to read. He opened the pages about my visit to Mount St Mary's Mission. 'You met the terrorists', he snarled as he kept reading. When he started to question me about my activities, I recalled the parting words of John Deary. 'I won't answer your questions until our lawyer arrives', I said. 'The longer you're silent, the longer you'll remain in prison', he responded. This was my first clue that I was going to be arrested rather than deported. 'Let's go to prison then', I replied.

The officers told me to pack a nightgown, tooth paste and soap as well as one change of clothes. I quickly put these in the Kenyan basket that I had brought with me and we went down the stairs of the flat and into the police car again. This time we went to the main police headquarters in downtown Harare where my fingerprints were taken and a photo. I felt like a character in one of the murder mysteries that I enjoyed reading. Back in the car, we drove out of Harare through a leafy green suburb where only white people were allowed to live. One of the policemen commented on how beautiful it was. Forgetting John Deary's wise words to remain silent, I replied that it was unfortunate that only white people lived in such comfortable surroundings while the Africans were forced to live in tiny houses close together in the townships. Defensively he responded that the African people in Rhodesia were treated better than those in any independent African country. This was a frequent refrain that I had heard before and I gave my standard response: 'How many other African countries have you been to'? I told him that I had been to many and that I couldn't agree that Africans were better off here. I told him that this was indeed a beautiful country but that it would be even better if the resources of the land could be shared equally between white and black. 'You're a communist', one of them said. I thought about this a minute and denied it. 'I think I'm a liberal', I said in reply. By now, the conversation was getting more tense and heated. When I asked one of the policemen what he thought about the war, he showed some anger as he declared, 'I'm not talking to you anymore because one day you'll probably write about it in a book'. If he ever reads these words written almost forty years later, I hope that he gets a laugh out of the fact that I did.

After about thirty minutes we arrived at the gates of Chikurubi Prison, a maximum-security facility on the outskirts of Harare where captured guerrillas and their sympathizers were held and sometimes hanged. The guards were expecting me and I was taken immediately to a building where I would be held for the next three weeks. I was led to a large room that contained an iron bedstead, a folding chair and a small table next to the bed. The floor was cement and there were two windows, looking out into a small courtyard. It was the month of August and freezing cold. I was given nothing to eat and was locked in and told that I wouldn't be allowed out until 5:00 the next morning when the guards unlocked the door and I was permitted to use the toilet further down the corridor.

I lay down on the lumpy bed and pulled a dirty grey blanket up to my shoulders. I shivered and curled into a ball to keep warm and wondered what would happen next. I finally fell asleep and was startled to hear the key turn in the lock the next morning. I was assigned two African guards, Bridget and Betty, to be with me at all times. It seems that I was considered a dangerous political prisoner. When the guards asked me why I was there, I couldn't really say but I told them that I worked with the CCJP. They were very friendly and wanted to know about life in Kenya since the Rhodesian media painted a grim picture of life in independent Africa. They also wanted to learn some Swahili and I asked them to teach me some Shona. They told me that I reminded them of Dr. Luisa, who had been arrested the previous year and detained in this same room for several days before she was released. She also supported liberation and was accused of medically treating the guerrillas. I was touched to be compared to such an outstanding missionary.

'When the guerrillas come to rescue you, tell them that we support them too', the African guards said. 'We only work here because we have to feed our children'. The prison was surrounded by trees and the African guards knew that the guerrillas were present in the Chishawasha Valley below. They firmly believed that one night the guerrillas would sneak up to the prison through the protective cover of the trees and release me and others being held.

I soon learned that hundreds of young women were being held there as well, accused of feeding the guerrillas or trying to join them. The prison was segregated in the same way as the rest of the country with different sections for white, black and colored prisoners. I was being held in the colored section, having displaced two colored women who were imprisoned and had been moved to the white section to make room for me. I was being kept apart since I was considered a dangerous political prisoner.

I learned just how dangerous one day when I overheard a radio broadcast declaring that I could be sentenced to death by hanging. Distraught that I had heard this news, the African guards ran to tell the head of the women's prison, Mrs Wright. She called me to her office and reassured me that things moved slowly through the judicial system and it was unlikely that my case would come to court before the war ended. She then surprised me by asking if I would like a sleeping pill, since she feared that the disturbing news bulletin might keep me awake. I was taken off guard by this unexpected kindness but refused the sleeping tablet. 'I never have any trouble sleeping', I assured her.

This wasn't entirely true. We were locked up so early that I often found myself waking in the middle of the night, needing to go to the bathroom. I discovered that there were no locks on the windows so I would climb out and make my way down the dark corridor to the toilets. Once I was almost caught when the guards with their flashlights and dogs made their rounds of the prison. I barely managed to climb through the window and curl under the covers when they shone the light through the window. I don't know what would have happened if they had found me missing.

The afternoon after my arrest, Mr Nick McNally, the lawyer for the Commission, was allowed to see me. He told me that they had had trouble locating me since the police pretended that they didn't know where I was. A phone call from a friend in the prison system alerted them to my whereabouts. Mr McNally told me that our conversation was probably being recorded so I should say as little as possible. He told me that I was being held indefinitely under the Law-and-Order Maintenance Act. Since I had just written a fact paper about this piece of legislation, I knew what it meant. Apparently, my diary as well as the short-wave radio that Brother Arthur had given me had raised suspicions. They suspected that I was in contact with guerrilla forces and giving them the location of army units and gleaning this from a special channel on the radio. I had no idea such a channel existed and was doing nothing more harmful or revolutionary than listening to the news on the BBC, Voice of America and the overseas service of Dutch Radio. Mr McNally also told me that the residences of Brother Arthur and Fr Scholz had been searched and it was likely that Fr Scholz would be deported. I was not cheered up by this news and returned to my big cold cell with little hope of leaving.

A more cheerful respite came several times a week when Fr

Ribeiro, the prison chaplain, brought me Holy Communion. Even though he could not stay long, his presence was very calming. I later learned that after these visits he called Sr Annette Mulry in the Global Concerns Office at the Maryknoll Sisters' Center in New York. She in turn phoned my parents in Pittsburgh to assure them that their daughter was fine. I later learned that my mother could not eat from worry and lost 10 pounds while I was in prison. She and my father were interviewed on Voice of America and told the world that they were proud of their daughter and also supported the end of minority rule in Rhodesia.

I was allowed two visitors while I was in Chikurubi. The Papal Nuncio came from South Africa and assured me that the Church was watching the situation and was concerned for my welfare. Mrs Wright, the head of the prison, sat in on the visit. Each time the Nuncio would ask me a question in his strong Italian accent, she would interrupt and tell me that I was not allowed to answer any question about the conditions in the prison or about my case. It was a comic routine as he persisted. 'How iz de bed?', he asked. 'Don't answer,' says Mrs Wright. 'It's fine,' I tell him. 'And de food? How iz de food?' 'Don't answer.' 'It's fine.' I don't know if he caught the humor in the situation but I was deeply touched that he had come from South Africa to see me and that the Vatican was following the case. I later learned that the Vatican Commission for Peace and Justice issued a statement in support of the CCJP in Rhodesia, calling for my release.

Another visitor allowed in with similar constraints on conversation was Sr Josephine Kollmer, our regional Maryknoll coordinator who was based in Kenya. Jo and I were old friends, having been in Kenya at the same time. We talked mainly about our Sisters in Kenya and Tanzania since Mrs Wright again censored any conversation about my present situation.

I had read somewhere that it was important to keep your mind active when you were in prison so I asked for a Bible so I could memorize it. The following day I was brought a stack of Bibles, of varying translations. I started by reading the Gospel of Mark since it was the shortest and I thought it would be the easiest to memorize. As I read the chapters about the life of Christ, it was as if I were reading it for the first time. From the very beginning, Mark recounts the cost of discipleship. On each page, Jesus is confronted with enemies who threaten and challenge him. It reminded me of the opposition that the Justice and Peace Commission faced from the Rhodesian government and from many Catholics, especially in Salisbury's mainly all-white parishes. Our Lady of the Wayside in Mt Pleasant was one such parish. The CCJP was asked repeatedly why we didn't condemn the terrorists? Why didn't the missionaries report their presence? Why did we expose only the atrocities committed by the Rhodesian forces? Why did we suspect that the Selous Scouts murdered the missionaries? It was a comfort to realize that Jesus and his disciples also faced fierce criticism from within their society and their church.

The Psalms were also very comforting as they speak of God's protection and guidance. 'God is my rock and my shield; I will fear no evil'. As I read them and the Gospels, I felt that they were written just for me. Each stanza and verse spoke of God's love and protection in times of trial. I read verses like, 'You, O God, are a shield for me...I cried to the Lord with my voice, and God heard me...sustained me.... I will not be afraid....' (Psalm 3). It also speaks of what will happen to enemies, 'For you have struck my enemies on the cheekbone; you have broken the teeth of the ungodly'! Really, that's what it says! Astonishing words when you are behind bars and don't know what those enemies have in store for you. Psalm 4 is equally consoling. 'Hear me when I call.... You have relieved me when I was in distress.... You have put gladness in my heart... I will both lie down in peace, and sleep, for you alone, O God, make me dwell in safety'. I could go through every psalm this way. Let me just share one more, as each is more powerful than the last. This is Psalm 7: 'O Lord my God, in You I put my trust, save me from all those who persecute me and deliver me, lest they tear me like a lion, rending me in pieces, while there is none to deliver'. While I didn't expect to be torn to pieces, I was told that I could face death by hanging for supporting 'terrorists'.

I wrote in my diary, 'I knew that God was with me in my cell'. Even though the bed was filthy and full of lumps, the food tasteless, the routine and lack of freedom monotonous and the uncertainty about the future frightening, I have never felt so peaceful and contented in my life. And as I wrote later in a little book about the wisdom we can learn from animals: 'God's love became as real as the air I breathed and the blood that coursed through my veins'.[1]

One finds ways around the rules in prison just as we found ways around the rules in the religious novitiate. I was soon introduced to the game of bartering. Our daily diet was very starchy and insubstantial but once a week we were given a piece of fruit, usually an orange, and a few cigarettes. One of the white prisoners who had been convicted of murdering her husband would give me her orange in exchange for my cigarettes. I readily agreed.

Once the African prisoners went on strike and refused to eat their main meal because they had seen one of the white guards burn some sanitary napkins in the fire under the cooking pots. This was a big taboo in their culture so they sat in silence and refused to eat that day. Another day, when they learned that I would eat African food, they managed to bring me a plate of sadza, a stiff porridge made from maize meal, with some vegetables. Another time, one of the African prisoners was sent to bring something to my guards. Prisca had been a young sister with the local LCBL community, headed by Sr Rocha, and I had met her previously. We were both

---

1 *Ostriches, Dung Beetles and Other Spiritual Masters: A Book of Wisdom from the Wild.* Orbis Books: New York (2009) p. 68.

surprised to meet again under these circumstances and she soon began to pass notes to me to tell me about the conditions of the women prisoners who slept crowded together on mats on the floor in a dormitory-like room. At night they sang freedom songs that rang out over the prison and lifted our spirits. This was probably forbidden but they never stopped singing. Since the three white women did not live on the prison grounds, they may never have learned about this act of defiance and the African guards may have joined in the singing.

On Sundays there were church services led by one of the Christian denominations. The services were held in a fenced enclosure opposite mine so I could see and hear everything. On one occasion the prisoners acted out the story of the two women who claimed the same baby. When they went to court, the wise judge decreed that the child should be cut in half. The real mother refused, as she would rather lose her child than see it killed. The women acted the story with great emotion and energy. They also sang rousing hymns and danced with joy. This was the one bright spot in a week of boring routine and forced obedience.

I asked for some work to do since memorizing the Bible could also be boring, even though the stories were very gripping and real. I was given the task of keeping an inventory of the food received and used from the prison farm and from outside suppliers. How could I have imagined that my first job before I joined Maryknoll of keeping an inventory in a motor parts shop would one day come in handy in a Rhodesian prison! I was also allowed to do gardening in my small courtyard, which brought back happy memories of working with my father in our small garden at our home in Pittsburgh. Finally, I was brought a sewing machine to make my prison uniform as the ones in stock were far too small for my five foot seven and a half inches. Again, how could I have imagined that my work in the sewing room at Maryknoll would be useful in a prison.

A week after my detention, I was brought my dress and told I was going to court. I was taken by surprise, not knowing why or what to expect. We went by prison van to the Harare Central Court on Rotten Row, across from Ranche House College where I had taken Shona lessons. I was put in a cell underneath the courtrooms as I awaited a visit from Nick McNally to tell me what was going on. While I waited, another prisoner coming for trial leaned down as if to tie her shoe when she was in front of my cell and said to me. 'Not only the church supports you but the whole country'. These whispered words of encouragement filled me with confidence and prepared me for what came next.

The CCJP lawyer, Nick McNally, entered the cell and told me that this was a hearing to see if I could be released on bail. He said that the government would probably use things I had written in my diary against me. 'You cannot be convicted for your thoughts', he said. 'You haven't done anything illegal'. Then he told me to say as little as possible and to let him do the talking. Once again, I ignored this wise advice. I felt that I had nothing to hide and should speak the truth.

Several guards escorted me up the stairs to the courtroom. I was shocked when I entered to find it packed with people as well as reporters with cameras. I was glad that I had been a fan of Perry Mason, a courtroom drama that had been popular on TV when I was growing up since it prepared me for the outward trappings of a legal tug of war. I was led to the dock and swore on a bible that I would tell the truth, the whole truth and nothing but the truth. Nick McNally feared that I would do exactly that. When the magistrate asked me for my name, I nervously replied in a small voice. He chided me to speak up. At that moment I recalled the Gospel passage where Jesus tells his followers not to worry about what to say when they are taken before judges for the Spirit will speak through them. I felt a surge of energy and all fear vanished. At the same time, so did my lawyer's wise counsel not to talk. Instead, I freely answered the questions I was asked. When the judge asked if I supported the terrorists, I replied that they were not terrorists but freedom fighters. Later, one of the guards who had accompanied me from the prison said, 'I wanted to clap when you wouldn't call them terrorists'. I recall that I used the theory of the 'just war' to explain why I was not disobeying the church's teaching when I supported the right of the majority to take up arms to gain their independence. At the end of the session, the judge said that I was a self-confessed supporter of terrorism and a communist. My lawyer's plea that 'thoughts were not a crime' went unheeded and I was taken back to prison having been denied bail.

Two weeks later, just as I had finished making my prison uniform and was modeling it to the guards, Mr McNally visited Chikurubi again to tell me that I would be deported the following day. I expressed regret and said that I wanted to stay and support the other members of the Justice and Peace Commission who were also fighting legal battles. 'They will be better off without you', were his parting words. Not very consoling but I understood what he meant.

The following morning, I was brought my dress again and told that I was leaving the prison. Somehow the other prisoners knew that I was leaving before I did and when my friend Prisca brought me my dress, she also brought me a handful of letters that the prisoners had written to tell of their plight. She asked me to get them into the hands of people who could help. I quickly hid them in the bottom of my Kenya bag. I barely had time to say good-by as I was bundled into a police car that would take me to the airport. I asked if I could stop by the Justice and Peace Office to say good-by. Amazingly, they agreed. We stopped first at a bank where I was given the little money, they had taken from me when I was arrested, to prove that they were honest. Brother Arthur was taken by surprise when I walked into his office. The police stayed outside so I gave Arthur the letters from the prisoners and told him he would know what to do with them. I was then taken to my flat where my suitcase was packed and ready to go. I learned that Sr Dymphna had come after I was arrested and cleared up everything.

At the airport, I waited with the police in a private room. After all the other passengers had walked up the stairway, the police opened the door and told me to go out and board the plane. As I climbed the stairs, I heard some singing coming from the balcony of the airport. I turned around and was overcome to see dozens of priests and sisters singing a hymn of farewell and waving to me. I was deeply touched by this public sign of support. A photographer caught me waving back. It is my favorite photo and I have asked that it be used on the program for my funeral. It is the photo that I chose for the cover of this book.

I rarely speak of one of the most significant spiritual experiences of my life that happened to me in Chikurubi Prison. I was shy to tell anyone about something so personal and so profound. Until today, it is something that comforts me and also puzzles me because it seems like something I made up or imagined and might give the wrong impression that I was a better person than I am. When I speak of my prison experience, I tease that it was like my novitiate – full of silence and rules. I never speak of the following experience for fear of being misunderstood or put on a pedestal.

A few nights after my detention, I started to go over in my head what I had written in my diary. I thought of all the people and places that I had mentioned and felt miserable that I had probably got them into trouble. Cold, scared and feeling foolish and guilty, I broke down sobbing and blaming myself for being so stupid and careless. As I lay sobbing on my hard, cold, dirty bed, a warm glow appeared in the right-hand corner of the room at the foot of the bed. The light grew brighter and moved closer to me. Then a voice came from the light, saying, 'You are the stupid, silly little girl who I love.' I felt an inner warmth and a sense of peace and safety as the light shown around me. Gradually the light began to recede and grow dimmer but the warmth and consolation stayed with me for the rest of my stay in Chikurubi and ever since.

I had been taught to be strong and self-reliant. I seldom showed my emotions and rarely asked for help, which I thought was a sign of weakness. I was capable and self-possessed and felt good about it. I seldom allowed myself to be vulnerable. Now when I was most alone, miserable and forsaken and all my defenses were down, God had visited me in my distress. I learned that in my weakness and fear, God had not abandoned me. I never again doubted God's love and protection although I continued to fear for the lives of others that I might have endangered.

10

A Bittersweet Homecoming

Ian Smith's government sent me to New York via South Africa, though I had hoped to return to Kenya and continue my work there. On the plane to Johannesburg, a woman reporter sat next to me and interviewed me. I doubt if anything I said made sense since I was still reeling from this rapid change of plans. I desired to remain in prison in solidarity with the hundreds of political prisoners throughout the country. I firmly believed that freedom would come within the next three years and that by then I would have completed my goal of memorizing the Bible!

I felt a failure who had got others into trouble. Fr Pascal Slevin and Sr Theresa Corby would both be deported, possibly because of what I had written in my diary. They later reassured me and told me that the deportation may have saved their lives since the Rhodesian Army raided the mission shortly after my arrest and closed it down. When they returned after the war was over, Pascal was proud to say that nothing had been stolen or removed from the community house. He believed that the guerrillas had guarded it against looting or vandalism. In fact, many of the guerrilla commanders came to visit him after Independence to thank him for his support.

I also learned that members of the Commission were obliged to defend me at all-white parishes where the Commission was already held suspect. Now the parishioners' worst fears had been confirmed - these men and women who preached equality and justice were communists who supported the terrorists. Members of the Commission tried to put out the fire and assure the parishioners that my words had been taken out of context.

To make matters worse, a few days after my deportation, the *Rhodesia Herald*, a pro-government newspaper, began to publish excerpts from my diary, accusing me of being a seeker after danger and somewhat mentally deranged. Mr McNally was called to the rescue again and the Commission's lawyers managed to stop any further use of my diary in this manner. At the same time, the Rhodesian government was embarrassed by all the publicity that I had received and the show of support by priests and sisters at the airport. They, therefore, passed a new law prohibiting photos or coverage of political trials and deportations. I joke that it should have been called 'McLaughlin's Law'.

On arrival in Johannesburg, I was surprised to find the U.S Ambassador waiting to greet me. He took me to a private lounge and warned me it was probably bugged. By now, I didn't care since I knew that I was not guilty of the accusations against me. I told him freely all that I had seen and experienced in my few months in the country. I can't recall if I slept on the flight to New York but when I arrived at JFK airport in the early hours of the morning, I went immediately to a telephone to call my sister Mary Ellen to let her know I was there. I was puzzled when the number rang repeatedly with no reply. I knew she was not an early riser and expected her to pick up and be surprised to hear my voice. I didn't call Maryknoll because I knew that the switchboard only opened at eight in the morning and it was only about six a.m. I thought no-one knew what had happened and was wondering how I would get to Maryknoll since I had very little money. I doubted that bus and taxi drivers in New York would give me a free ride as had those in Rhodesia.

When I proceeded out of the arrival's hall, I was overcome to find a big crowd waiting for me, including my sister Mary Ellen and Sister Barbara Hendricks, the President of our congregation. I fell into their arms with surprise and relief. I had no idea that the major news and TV outlets had covered my deportation as well as my day in court. I was flabbergasted to learn that I had been in the headlines and that my plight had been broadcast nationally.

We drove straight to Maryknoll where the Sisters at our Center were waiting in the chapel to welcome me with prayers of Thanksgiving. One of the senior sisters learned over and whispered in my ear: 'We're so proud of you. If I was your age, I would have done the same thing.' I was moved by her understanding and affirmation of what I had done since I still felt as if I had let down the other members of the Commission and had not been able to see them to discuss what it all meant. Aside from Brother Arthur, I had not been able to talk to a single member of the Commission nor to my good friend Sr Dymphna since no one was allowed to visit me in prison.

The day was a whirlwind of interviews by various reporters that had been arranged by our Communications Office. Sr Elizabeth Roach, another Pittsburgher, had recently taken over the office and joked that this was her baptism by fire! That evening, I gave a briefing to our entire community in one of our large classrooms. I spoke from the heart of all that I had seen and heard in my few months on the frontline of this country at war and shared stories of the amazing people of courage and faith that I had met. Unfortunately, no record remains of this talk.

I was taken upstairs to one of the small rooms to sleep. The tension and stress of the last few weeks had built up within me and I began to shiver and to shake uncontrollably. I was freezing cold and asked for more blankets. Someone brought me a heating pad and possibly a sleeping pill as well. Gradually I fell into a deep slumber, my first night in a proper bed for more than three weeks.

I found it hard to adjust to my new situation. I felt lost and adrift and worried constantly about my companions who I had left behind. Had I made things worse for them, I wondered? Would I be condemned for putting them into danger? I felt as if there was no-one to whom I could turn who would understand what I had experienced. Sr Maria Rieckelman, one of our Sisters who was a psychiatrist, and very wise woman, came to see me. In her no-nonsense manner, she told me to have faith in myself and in the colleagues that I had left behind. They would be able to take care of themselves. She absolved me from feeling I had failed and that I was responsible for the fate of others, but I still struggled with what I should do now.

A week or so later, I flew to Pittsburgh to see my parents who met me at the airport together with Fr Bryce, Diocesan Director for the Missions and a friend of my family. Photographers were also at the airport to meet me and made me realize that I was no longer a private person who could be anonymous. I was a minor celebrity in my home town and was invited to give talks by various groups. I learned that the Association of Pittsburgh Priests, a progressive group of priests, had supported me as well as the staff and members of the Thomas Merton Center, the local equivalent of the Justice and Peace Commission in Rhodesia. These two groups were kindred spirits and would become life-long friends and supporters. Molly Rush, the Director of the Merton Center, would herself be imprisoned three years later, when she entered a nuclear weapons plant in Eastern Pennsylvania with others, who became known as the Plowshares Eight, and hammered the nosecones of nuclear missiles.

Some African students from Rhodesia who were studying at local universities came to see me and recruit me to their cause. They had come to the United States through the offices of Bishop Abel Muzorewa, a member of the Internal Settlement with Ian Smith. Once they were enrolled in college, they quickly switched sides and joined ZANU, thereby endangering their scholarships and their right to remain in the United States. They also sought my support for a campaign against local steel companies that were violating international sanctions against Rhodesia by importing chrome and other minerals.

As I got embroiled in these local issues, I became controversial and my hero status faded fast. Hate letters started to arrive at our home, calling me all kinds of names, some of them smeared with fecal matter. One day a rock was thrown at our front window, causing my mother to speak words of deep wisdom. 'You better go back to Africa', she said. 'When you speak out against injustice there, you are a hero. When you do it here, you're just a trouble maker'. With these few sentences, she accurately summed up the hypocrisy, double standards and racism of many Americans towards action for peace and justice at home and abroad.

11

In the Belly of the Beast:
The Washington Office on Africa

I intended to follow my mother's advice and return to East Africa when I received another unexpected invitation. Ted Lockwood, Director of the Washington Office on Africa (WOA), an ecumenical advocacy group based in Washington DC, asked me to join the office to work on issues related to Rhodesia. In the first few months after my deportation, I had been going on speaking tours with Zimbabweans based in the States to explain the situation in that country and to lobby for a retention of sanctions and support for the liberation movements of ZANU and ZAPU. Tirifavi Kangai and Callistus Ndlovu, the respective representatives of these two movements in the United States, reached out to me and encouraged me to continue to speak to various groups, including some of the small leftist groups in the States.

This steady diet of travelling nationwide and speaking about what I had seen and experienced in Rhodesia was taking a toll on me. I was exhausted and feeling rundown and depressed. I didn't see that these talks were making any difference and I was more and more isolated from my Maryknoll community. Ted's invitation opened another door and probably saved me from total burnout.

My years in Kenya and the short time that I had spent in Rhodesia, had convinced me that the foreign policy of the U.S. government was often ill-conceived and counter-productive. From our members in Central and South America, I had learned how the US often supported corrupt dictators rather than those who it considered were leftists or communists, even though they had been chosen by their own people. I knew of similar cases on the African continent. In the Congo, for instance, Patrice Lumumba, the first African President, was executed and replaced by a corrupt military leader, Mobutu Sese Seko, with help from the CIA. Ghana was another example where Kwame Nkrumah, the first president, was overthrown with the help of the CIA, leading to years of instability and military control.

I moved to Washington DC with a jaundiced view of my country's foreign policy and ignorant of how the government worked. The months that I spent with WOA were a crash-course in citizen participation and the ways that one could influence foreign policy as well as how to mobilize popular support. Ted Lockwood and Christine Root, his colleague, were patient teachers as they led me through the intricacies of how a bill becomes law and the steps along the way where citizens can exert influence. I accompanied them to congressional hearings like the one at which I had testified four years previously. We visited congressional offices, leaving information about the issues under discussion and met with the aides who were usually young, well-intentioned and eager to learn. The staff of the Senate Foreign Relations Committee and the House Committee on International Affairs were particularly influential and gave us useful tips on how best to proceed and told us who were our allies on Capitol Hill and who were the opponents.

Tip O'Neill, speaker of the House, was the nephew of our Sr Eunice and valued the knowledge and experience of Maryknoll. He helped to pave the way for me to meet others who shared my outlook and concerns about the future of Rhodesia. I met so many dedicated and sincere Senators and Congress people that it's impossible to name them all and to do them justice. This stint on Capitol Hill gave me a new appreciation of the U.S. government and the various arms that help make it work. While I sometimes became discouraged at the tendency to view most issues through the lens of how they would benefit the United States, I learned to do this without diluting the message in which I believed. I was called to testify again at a congressional hearing on whether to lift sanctions against Rhodesia in light of the changes that were taking place inside the country with the internal settlement between Ian Smith and three African leaders.

With the help of Ted and Chris, I prepared my testimony and delivered it with confidence. Our argument was that the changes were only cosmetic and that the war would not end without bringing in all parties to the conflict, meaning the liberation movements, ZANU and ZAPU. I quoted documents of the Justice and Peace Commission and gave examples from my own experience. After being questioned in a Rhodesian courtroom, this seemed tame by comparison. When it came time for questions, however, I learned that my dubious reputation had followed me. Senator Jesse Helms of North Carolina and Senator Hayakawa of California both ganged-up to challenge me and to cast doubts on my reputation. At one point, Senator Hayakawa read a report from a Tanzanian newspaper, quoting my diary, in which I had written, 'If I had a black skin, I would join the 'boys', the *vakomana* in Shona, the affectionate name by which the guerrillas were known. He then looked at me and said, 'This sounds rather blood-thirsty for a bride of the Prince of Peace'. The whole chamber burst into laughter. There was no further need for me to respond.

When I left the high table, Cyrus Vance, former Secretary of State under President Carter who resigned as a matter of conscience over Operation Eagle Claw, the secret mission to rescue American hostages in Iran, stopped me to thank me and to let me know that he fully supported my position. He was not alone and the bill to lift sanctions was defeated. Interestingly enough, it was the mining companies operating in Rhodesia that had helped to sway the vote in our favor. They realized that unless the liberation movements were involved in talks, the war would not end and the war was crippling their business.

In Washington I was surrounded by like-minded people who were tireless in their efforts to obtain justice in various parts of the world. One of our Sisters, Peg Healey, often testified for the Washington Office on Latin America (WOLA) in relation to the situation in Nicaragua and El Salvador. I lived with a former Maryknoll Sister who had worked with me in the communications office at Maryknoll and had been my roommate at Marquette. Mary Lou Reker and I were kindred spirits who had stayed up late writing term papers in college, marched arm and arm down the streets of Milwaukee for racial justice, and now put our heads together to find creative ways to lobby Congress. In the background, Sr Annette Mulry at our Office for Global Concerns in New York continued to give me good advice and to keep the links with Maryknoll strong and relevant.

As the war continued to escalate and more lives were lost, diplomatic efforts to find a political settlement increased. The CCJP was deeply involved in these initiatives. Our 'fact papers' about the war had made an impact in London and in DC. They were published in a booklet, *Rhodesia the Propaganda War,* while I was still in prison and circulated widely, giving lawmakers an insight into the situation on the ground in Rhodesia. Members of the Commission were called on to give briefing to the Vatican Commission for Peace and Justice and were invited to testify in Washington. With support from the Catholic Institute for International Relations, WOA was able to bring three members of the Justice and Peace Commission to Washington to testify at another round of hearings.

To my great joy, I was reunited with Mr John Deary, the chairman, and Brother Fidelis Mukonori SJ, who I had last seen at the fateful meeting when the police came to take me to prison. Mr Mike Auret was also with them. He had joined the Commission after I had left. As a former white farmer, he knew the thinking of white Rhodesians and was able to speak from another point of view. This trio stopped at Maryknoll after their visit to Washington and gave a briefing to our Sisters. I was so proud and happy to be connected to such courageous and faith-filled people. Mike especially impressed me as he spoke of growing up as a white person and not believing that Africans were fully human. His attitude had only changed when he interacted with the workers on the farm where he lived and learned that they had the same hopes and dreams for their children as he did for his. His honest admission of being a racist touched those who heard him speak and perhaps helped us to get in touch with our own racism, growing up in North America.

A phone call came that evening for Mr Deary after this session with the sisters. It was from his wife in Salisbury, telling him that a grenade had been thrown through their bedroom window but had failed to go off, probably sparing her life. We went into the chapel at Maryknoll to pray for Pat Deary and for all those facing violence in that war torn country. Although none of us slept well that night, they were up early the next morning for appointments in New York City.

The Commission members made a big impact in Washington and helped convince the members of Congress that an all-party conference was necessary to end the war. I was invigorated by this international outreach and felt at home in the halls of Congress. In fact, I used to speculate that if I hadn't become a Maryknoll Sister, I might have run for political office and become the first woman Senator from Pennsylvania! Although I thrived in this environment and realized that these diplomatic and political interventions were necessary, I yearned to be closer to the action on the African continent. I didn't have long to wait.

12

A *Luta Continua*: with Refugees in Mozambique

When I returned to Maryknoll after the congressional hearings, I received a call from CIIR in London. 'Would you like to go to Mozambique?' It was Mildred Neville, head of CIIR and she was opening a door to a new and challenging experience. She explained that the churches had set up an organization, the Zimbabwe Project, to assist refugees in Zambia and Mozambique who had fled the war in their home country. The liberation movements had agreed to endorse this initiative. Fr Michael Traber, my friend who had been deported from Rhodesia, was sent to meet with Robert Mugabe in Maputo. He received an enthusiastic welcome but was told that the liberation movements would not allow anyone to enter the refugee camps. After the attacks on two camps, Nyadzonia and Chimoio, by Rhodesian forces that killed many women and children, they feared disclosing information about the sites of the camps. Spies were everywhere and trust was very low. Finally, they came to an agreement. 'We will allow Sr. Janice to visit our camps'.

When I received the invitation from CIIR, I again knew instinctively that this was my call. Without hesitation, I approached our President, Sr Barbara Hendricks, who had met me at the airport in New York when I was deported. She readily agreed. 'If you are needed, you should go'. I rejoiced at her understanding and support. I often tell people that she didn't ask me where I would stay or if I would be near a church or convent and have access to Mass and the sacraments. 'If you are needed', was her only criteria. I found such trust very liberating and empowering. There was no way that I would let her down.

Within a few weeks I was on my way to Maputo with little idea of what I would find there or what I would actually be doing. Fortunately, or providentially, I had visited Mozambique the previous year with a group of so-called 'progressive Americans'. We had been recruited by Robert van Lierop, well-known film-maker and lawyer, who had made a film about Frelimo's liberation struggle, *A Luta Continua*, that had won him the trust and sympathy of the new government in Mozambique and its first President, Samora Machel.

He took twelve of us from different professions and different parts of the United States to gain exposure to this country in southern Africa that called itself Marxist and was off limits to most Americans. My aunt Ruth Casey paid for my ticket. Although she was critical of Mozambique's ideology, she never questioned my intentions and I knew I could count on her to help me.

What struck me about this country was the humility of those who were our guides, most of them working in the Ministry of Information in the FRELIMO government. Without exception, they began their talks by saying, 'We have many problems'. They went on to enumerate the poverty, destruction of infrastructure by the departing Portuguese settlers, and the hostility of the neighboring countries, Rhodesia and South Africa. Then they would show us what they had been able to accomplish in spite of these obstacles. We saw schools, hospitals, rural clinics, fishing cooperatives, a glass blowing factory, steel mill and harbor. We were taken to a refugee camp of Zimbabweans in the center of the country and, when we returned to Maputo, we watched a horrifying film of the brutal attack on the refugees at Chimoio by Rhodesian forces. The Mozambican army had been the first on the scene after this raid on the camp. A filmmaker accompanied them and photographed the dozens of bodies thrown into mass graves, others still scattered throughout the camp, and interviewed a woman who had survived by hiding in a pit latrine. She was deeply traumatized and could barely speak. I left the small theatre even more committed to do whatever I could to hasten the end of the war and to assist the refugees.

The invitation from CIIR was an answer to prayer. When I returned to Maputo under the auspices of the Zimbabwe Project, various leaders of ZANU welcomed me and assured me of their support and cooperation in my new ministry. I needed it since the refugee camps were under the authority of the liberation movement.

The night of my arrival, Simon Muzenda, the Vice President of ZANU and a devoted Catholic, came to see me at the flat of Roberta Washington, an American architect who was working in Mozambique as a *cooperante*. The FRELIMO government welcomed international solidarity from individuals who supported their freedom, even if their governments were hostile to FRELIMO because of its Marxist orientation. I soon came to know many of the *cooperantes* who were doing incredible work under difficult circumstances and I stayed with some of them.

Comrade Muzenda (I learned to call everyone comrade since it was the normal title used during the war and one of respect. The Mozambicans were called the Portuguese equivalent or *camarada*.)

had brought along Tendie Ndlovu, a young Zimbabwean journalist who worked in ZANU's information department, so she could tell me her story. She had been one of the students abducted by ZANLA guerrillas from St Albert's, a Catholic mission school in the north-east of Zimbabwe in 1973. The Rhodesian army went in hot pursuit after this daring raid, capturing most of the students when they were crossing the Zambezi Valley. Tendie was one of only seven who completed the journey to Mozambique and joined the ZANLA forces. I would later do extensive research on this first major incident at a Catholic mission and made it one of four case studies in my PhD thesis at the University of Zimbabwe in 1992.

Simon Muzenda became a life-long friend and a person I could count on whenever I needed a higher authority to intercede for me. In Maputo, he sometimes invited me to join him and others for lunch at the house where he stayed. FRELIMO had given ZANU some houses in the capital to be used either as homes for the leaders or as offices. ZANU had its headquarters on the 11th floor of a large apartment complex in Maputo, overlooking the ocean. I became very familiar with these offices and paused to catch my breath half way up the stairs. I heard that Robert Mugabe never paused as he ran to the top of the building without stopping. He kept fit and neither drank alcohol nor smoked. It was rumoured that he woke early, did calisthenics, and meditated each morning before going to the office, a regime carried over from his years in prison. I respected this discipline and commitment.

One particular lunch at the home of Simon Muzenda can never be erased from my memory since it was so embarrassing and yet funny. I usually ate with some of the young recruits who were working in the various offices. On this occasion, I encountered ZANU's top military officers and heads of departments who had come to Maputo for a meeting. I caught my breath and tried to look calm as they sat me beside General Tongogara, head of the ZANLA forces. Vice President Muzenda was at the head of the table and Dzingai Mutumbuka, Secretary for Education, was seated across from me. There were several other leading figures seated around me, whose names I forget but they all welcomed me and knew who I was and why I was there.

When the meal was brought to the table, I was even more overwhelmed since it was my least favorite food – *matumbu* (cow's stomach), sadza and *derere* (okra). As the young comrades serving the meal piled my plate high, I suggested that it should go to Tongogara since he was the guest of honor. Looking at me with a straight face he said, 'We made it especially for you'. Everyone laughed since they knew it was a treat for him. My ordeal was not over. After the basin of water was passed to each person to wash our hands, I waited to see if the others would use the silverware that was at each place or whether they would use their fingers, which was the traditional Shona way of eating. All eyes were on me as they waited to see what I would do. Those few seconds were like a lifetime as I debated within whether to use my hands or a fork. I knew the food was steaming hot and I would burn my fingers and thought that maybe the silverware had been put there just for me. After what seemed like a lifetime of indecision, I picked up the fork and started to eat. When Dzingai Mutumbuka also picked up a fork. I relaxed and was deeply grateful that he sensed my unease and joined me, helping me to feel less of an outsider since every other person around the table used their fingers to eat.

After the meal, Dzingai took me aside to question me about my motives for coming to Mozambique and working with ZANU. I knew that he had been raised a Catholic, had a doctorate in science from Trinity College in Ireland, and was a good friend of Fr Traber and the Bethlehem Fathers. I was taken aback, therefore, when his questioning seemed hostile and made me feel as if I were facing Senators Helms and Hayakawa once again. 'How can a Catholic

Sister support Marxist guerrillas'? he asked, 'Isn't this against your religion'? I felt intimidated but answered him as honestly as I could, telling him about my experience with the Justice and Peace Commission inside the country and my conviction that the armed struggle was necessary to free the country from white minority rule. I think I also said that Catholic Sisters were often ahead of the bishops and the Pope. I must have passed the test for he laughed his hearty laugh and invited me to work in the Education Department of ZANU in Maputo, taking me to the office in a nearby house to meet the staff. Later, he arranged for me to visit the Education Headquarters in Matenje Camp in northern Mozambique where he spent most of his time.

At the Education office I was introduced to Comrades Ropa and Vimbisai, who would become close friends and colleagues. Ropa Rinopfuka (whose real name was Irene Mahamba) was a Catholic from Basera in Gutu while Vimbisai (Gertrude Nyakupinda) was the daughter of a catechist from the Zambezi Valley. They were writing and publishing textbooks for the schools in the camps that would later be used in independent Zimbabwe. I was in awe of these young, capable women who had left their homes and sacrificed their education for the hardships of the war. I did whatever was needed in the office such as photocopying, running errands or making tea. I had no special talents to offer and was just happy to be a part of this dedicated team.

After a few weeks of working in the Education office and visiting the other departments of ZANU to find out their needs, a trip was arranged for me to visit the camps in the north of the country. These were off limits, as mentioned above, to all other aid agencies including UNHCR and the World Food Programme. I felt very humbled and grateful to be so trusted. I flew from Maputo to Beira, a coastal city on the Indian Ocean, only a few hours by road from the border with Rhodesia. From there I was taken further north by plane to Tête Province and spent the night in a house that was used by General Tongogara and Josiah Tungamirai, the chief Political Commissar, when they were not at the front. I never met them there, since they spent most of their time within the country leading the troops but I got to know the young staff who assisted them. Every young person that I met was friendly, hardworking, and fun to be with. They made jokes of the hardships they had to endure and worked long hours, filing the reports that were sent by the commanders at the front and also doing reconnaissance trips inside Rhodesia. They often returned early in the morning after walking the entire night along the border area to report on the situation. I marveled at their endurance and their good humor.

Finally, the day came when they had a truck that could take me even further north into the forests where two of the largest refugee camps were located. Mavudzi Camp housed adults while Matenje, only a few miles away, was home to children, who were attending school under the trees.

The few weeks that I spent at Matenje Camp were like a crash course in living the Gospel. I slept in a thatched house with about a dozen children. The bed was made of sticks with a mattress of straw and a few blankets for the cold winter months of June, July and August. This bed was luxury compared to my bed in Chikurubi Prison. Instead of solitary confinement, dozens of children kept me company throughout the night and during the day. They seemed to have a sixth sense for when I needed to be alone and when I craved company. They would mysteriously disappear without my asking and then reappear when I was ready to converse. At sunrise each morning, they went to the river to bathe but I had the luxury of bathing in a small bucket of water that had been warmed. I also didn't join them for the early morning jog through the woods and would be woken by the singing as they practiced military drills and warmed up after a night that brought frost on the ground.

I had one small suitcase with me that contained a pair of jeans, a floppy hat, a few t-shirts, a sweater, a bar of soap and a comb. These few possessions became the playthings of my housemates. I cringed each time I came back to the thatched hut and found them trying on my clothes and using the comb. This seemed like an invasion of privacy to me but I quickly learned that in their culture there is no such thing as mine. Everything was ours and was for the use of all. I got used to it and was pleasantly surprised to find that each and every item was carefully replaced in the suitcase each day and put under my bed, just as they found it.

Comrade Ropa explained to me the communal nature of material goods in Shona culture. 'We never say my or mine but ours', she told me. 'We share whatever we have'. I saw this in action as the teachers who received gifts of food from senior commanders who were their partners or boyfriends would call me to their simple huts to give me a coke or a piece of sugarcane after the visits of those in command.

Ropa would laugh long and hard each time she found me 'counting'. When offered bananas, I would usually say, 'I'll take one'. To a soft drink, I might say, 'Give me half a cup'. She found this very hilarious and asked why I measured everything I was given. 'I want to save some for tomorrow, when we will have nothing', I told her. 'How will you feel when you are the only one who has anything', she countered? I said I thought we all should be saving. 'When we have something to eat or drink, we take it and enjoy it together', she said. 'Tomorrow, when there is nothing, we will all have nothing together'.

Something clicked in my head as I realized that I had grown up worrying about myself only and making sure that I had enough to eat, drink and wear. I seldom worried or thought about my sister or my parents and thought that they could take care of themselves. This kind of independence is valued in the US culture but it is considered selfish in a culture of scarcity where sharing is the norm. Without such an attitude, a few might thrive while the rest would starve. While such an attitude could lead to laziness, dependence or cheating, I could see the wisdom in the harsh conditions of the refugee camp.

In fact, we were almost facing starvation as the rations from the World Food Programme had not yet arrived. We lived on tinned salmon from North Korea and on the dried fish or kapenta that came in big sacks from the surrounding African states. The first time I was given a few of the little fish or sardines, I waited to see how to eat them. I watched in dismay as the teachers swallowed the fish whole, eyes, head and all. I summoned up my courage to do the same but could never get more than a few down my throat. We also had a small portion of sadza and some greens that were grown in the fields surrounding the camp.

I ate with the teachers in an open-air thatched hall, lit by rags in tin cans that were saturated with oil. At the end of the meager meal, we would stand outside under the stars and talk about every topic imaginable. These young recruits read widely and had a huge interest in international affairs. They grilled me about American politics and shared their theories about subjects as wide-ranging as the cultural revolution in China to drug trafficking in Colombia. I was fascinated by their knowledge and enjoyed these evening soirees that could match any college seminar course that I had ever attended.

For my enjoyment, the commanders sometimes organized evening entertainment by groups of students. They performed traditional songs and dances, recited poetry and acted out plays in a clearing near the dining hall. Sundays these entertainments replaced a church service as we gathered in a big clearing and each dormitory of students performed. At the first such gathering

I attended, the commander in charge of the camp introduced me to the students. The person sitting next to me poked me in the ribs and whispered, 'Stand up and shout slogans'. I was taken aback but had observed a few others who had spoken before me. I rose and with a clenched fist in the air shouted, 'Pamberi ne chimurenga'. (Forward with the armed struggle.) 'Pasi ne nyope'. (Down with laziness.) I later regretted that I didn't get up and join in the dancing but I was still shy and not entirely at home in this completely new environment.

Dzingai Mutumbuka had encouraged me to bring a camera and take pictures in the camps so that there would be a visual record of the educational work that was going on. Every day I walked to the various classes under the trees and took some photos of the desks and benches made out of local bamboo and of the student teachers who were totally engrossed in their lessons. Fay Chung, a Chinese Zimbabwean, who had taught in local township schools inside the country and at the University of Zambia before she came to Mozambique, was in charge of the teacher training program. She taught political economy as well as organizational development, using examples from the camps. One assignment that she gave was to design a system to keep the pit latrines clean and insect-free. Another was to design a system to prevent theft of plates and cups in the camp.

George Mandipaza (known as Cde Hakuzari) was in charge of the stores and under his watch I doubt if a single spoon went missing. He and I worked together after Independence and I have rarely met anyone so honest, unassuming, intelligent and humble – a delightful combination!

In the camps there was a system of bartering, just as there had been in prison. The refugees had a very dull, monotonous and meager diet so they would sometimes exchange the blankets or clothing that they received from the UNHCR or from overseas supporters for a chicken, a piece of sugarcane or a cigarette from local Mozambicans. It was understandable. Life was hard and dangerous. These small 'luxuries' brought a little relief into the routine although if they were caught, they would be punished.

Fay invited me to teach a class in journalism to the teacher trainees. I admired her ability to be at home in this demanding and dangerous environment. Her daughter Chipo was everyone's darling. She followed me around the camp and entertained me with Shona songs and dances. Much later Fay told me: 'I trusted you because Chipo did. Children have an ability to distinguish who is a friend'.

The student teachers were eager to learn and entered wholeheartedly into the lessons. I recall that I used an exercise that I had developed in Kenya to help students analyze the news and to distinguish facts from propaganda. They took a news item and rewrote it from the viewpoint of various media outlets ranging from Voice of Zimbabwe (ZANLA's nightly radio broadcast on Mozambican radio), Voice of America, the BBC, South African and Rhodesian channels. We looked together at the language used such as 'terrorists' versus 'freedom fighters' or 'guerrillas'; who are presented as the victims and who as the oppressors; what is added or omitted.[1] This lesson eventually ended up in Training for Transformation, a series of training manuals that put Paulo Freire's philosophy of education into practice. They were compiled by my old friends Anne Hope and Sally Timmel.

I had the students work on a camp newsletter with each of them taking a topic such as the health care in the camp or the lives of the local Mozambicans in the area. We were very proud when the newsletter was edited and published and we gave a copy to each of the teachers in the program as well as the camp commanders. The following day I was called to a meeting with

---

1 Hope A. and Timmel, S. (1984) *Training for Transformation*, Book III, Mambo Press, Gweru, p. 64.

the commanders. They gently explained that this newsletter must be destroyed and we could start over and write another. I was puzzled because I thought each of the contributions had been well researched and written. One of the commanders explained, 'If this fell into the hands of the Rhodesians or South Africans, they would use it to show that there was a rift between us and the people of Mozambique. They would allege that the Zimbabweans looked down on their Mozambican neighbors'. With this in mind, I reread our humble offering and saw that the description of the life of rural Mozambicans was indeed depicted as what might be termed backward and extremely poor. It seemed to suggest that Independence in Mozambique had not yet reached these remote villages and that some people had never heard of the government and were completely cut off from health or education. In fact, the articles suggested that the refugees were better off than their hosts.

We went back to the drawing board and compiled another newsletter, being much more careful of what we wrote. In a sense, we were learning in practice that what we wrote could be used as propaganda if it fell into the wrong hands, even though we thought it was factual. War changes one's perceptions and opens one's eyes to the reality.

I was also taken to Mavudzi, the nearby camp for adults where I shared a bed with one of the senior women commanders, Comrade Mabel. As I huddled under the flimsy blankets, I was kept awake by the noise of animals moving about on the floor. I jerked up when something landed on my head. Mabel laughingly told me that it was rats, coming down from the thatched roof to eat the crumbs that were on the floor. I put my head under the blankets and stopped counting the number of times that the rats jumped down onto the bed!

The first night I was in Mavudzi, I heard singing and dancing at a distance. The next morning, I was told that the spirit mediums who lived on the edges of the camp had held a service to consult the spirits of the ancestors about my presence. In Shona culture, the *zvikuru* or *vana sekuru* were highly esteemed and were considered guardians at the camps to warn against danger. During the war, the guerrillas called upon them for protection. These traditional spiritual leaders reminded the guerrillas of the moral dictates of the ancestors – no unnecessary shedding of blood, no killing of animals unless for food, no cutting down of trees, and no taking advantage of women. Some of these rules were contained in the guidelines that each member of the ZANLA forces memorized and sang at rallies.

The morning after my arrival at Mavudzi, I was told that the spirits of the ancestors had communicated that I was a friend and to be welcomed. This affirmation helped to pave the way for my acceptance. I wondered what would have happened had they rejected me! I learned much later that General Tongogara had also paved the way for me by writing a letter to all the commanders, explaining who I was and ordering them to assist me. My stay in the camps revealed the nature of the hardships endured as well as the attitude of self-reliance that helped to overcome them and to create a spirit of hope and even joy. I wrote about this in a report to the CIIR and the international donors who sent support through the Zimbabwe Project.

When I returned to Maputo after this incredible experience, I wrote to London listing the many needs in the camps. At the top of the list was anti-malaria medication since death by malaria was an even greater killer than the Rhodesian army. I also ordered plastic tubs for bathing the babies who were born in the camps as well as soccer balls for the children. While other aid agencies focused on food and clothing, these small additions to their lives, made the difference between endurance and resilience.

The funds raised in Europe were sent to the Catholic Church

in Swaziland that was then led by a revolutionary local bishop, Mandlekosi Zwane. Amazingly, he had been one of my journalism students at the All Africa Conference of Churches training center in Nairobi. He was appointed bishop while a student there. At the party we held to celebrate his promotion, he dressed in native Swazi attire – a bright colored cloth wrapped around the body leaving one shoulder bare – and awed us all with traditional local dances that featured stomping and kicking. What a contrast, I thought, to the staid bishops that I had known in Pittsburgh and New York.

I stayed at the bishop's residence in Mbabane and his director of refugees, Fr Somers, took me shopping at the large warehouses that were stocked with goods from South Africa. Mrs Dorothy Shamuyarira, a nurse married to Nathan, one of ZANU's leaders who had studied and taught in the States, accompanied me and helped to select the medicines that we would take back. With our shopping completed, Fr Somers drove us to the border in the diocesan truck where we were met by another truck sent by ZANU. At that time, the freedom fighters would be arrested if they set foot in Swaziland since it was still closely connected to apartheid South Africa and was crawling with secret agents. The goods were then taken to Maputo where they had to be cleared by customs. This was the most frustrating part of the entire process but thanks to the ingenuity of several young comrades who spoke fluent Portuguese, the goods were usually released after a few weeks and then sent north to the camps.

I was overjoyed when I next visited Matenje to see the students lined up to receive their weekly dose of malaria medication; the babies splashing in the brightly colored plastic tubs and the youth kicking the soccer balls on the playing field. But the greatest feat of all was in securing a large truck to transport goods and people to and from the camps. In all my meetings with the various heads of ZANU departments, I was told that this was a priority since they couldn't divert military vehicles to carry the supplies to the refugees, including food. The aid agencies in Europe were skeptical of this request, fearing that the truck could be used to ferry weapons and soldiers. When the new twenty-ton Benz truck finally arrived from Swaziland laden with supplies it was christened 'Sister Janice'. This was the first and only time that anything was named after me! That it was a twenty-ton truck made for many jokes. 'This is the REAL Sr Janice', was how I was introduced in the camps on my next visit. For years after that, I was thanked for obtaining this truck that was used even after the war was over to transport the children back home to Zimbabwe and to help bring supplies to the holding camps where they were staying. This was a battle with the donors that I was happy we had won.

When I was in Maputo I stayed with Josef Pampalk and Mary Salat. She had been a Maryknoll Sister and worked in Tanzania where she met her future husband who was a priest working in one of the ujaama villages. I became godmother to their first child Elias who was born in Maputo. They stayed in an apartment not far from the school where they taught. At that time food was very scarce in Maputo and we would jump in any queue that formed on the street, hoping that we would receive a loaf of bread or some rolls. These used to be plentiful before South Africa began its campaign to destabilize the newly independent government of Mozambique, cutting off goods from reaching the people. During the months that I was there, we survived on avocados that grew plentifully on the trees and the bread that we could obtain by waiting hours in the queues. Occasionally we used our scarce US dollars to shop in the international store where we could buy canned goods and other food. I learned that these international stores were common in socialist countries and catered for diplomats and aid agencies. Mary, Josef and I cringed at this inequality but we occasionally took advantage of it when we couldn't get any bread.

While in the city, I used my journalism background to interview various leaders in ZANU, including Robert Mugabe and General Tongogara. I found Robert Mugabe very personable and eager to speak about his Catholic upbringing and the similarity that he saw between the demands of his faith and the goals of the liberation struggle. *Southern Africa*, a magazine in the States that focused on the region, published this and other interviews that I did. They were also published in *Zimbabwe News*, put out by ZANU.

General Tongogara and I had already met as mentioned above. He was at ease and very articulate. I tried to be a proper journalist and not let my respect for him overcome my desire to ask hard-hitting questions. I recall that I asked him about the rumours that there were divisions between the political and military leaders. He avowed that he was the obedient son of the political leaders and repeated the slogan – 'Politics Rules the Gun'. Somehow, I doubted if this was the case since the political leaders were far from the frontline where the fighting was and the military leaders seldom came to Maputo to brief them. This was before the days of email and other electronic means of communication and in any event, they lived in the bush far from any telephones or fax machines. Electricity was very rare in this large country, recently liberated from Portuguese rule. I did not get the sense that there was tension between the political and military leaders, only that they had very different roles to play.

Josiah Tungamirai, ZANU's Chief Political Commissar, was present for the interview with Tongogara so I took advantage of this to interview him as well. I had learned from Fr Traber that he had been in the seminary and was an active Catholic before joining the struggle. He was very open and explained that his participation in freeing the country from colonial rule was not in contradiction to his religious beliefs but was in fact their fulfillment. He had a quick sense of humor and teased me about my own participation in the struggle and mixing with Marxists. 'What will the Pope say?', he asked. We all laughed.

Another interview was with Joice Mujuru, one of the first women to join the struggle. I met her at a center that ZANU had set up to teach practical skills to women. It was to serve as a prototype for the future. I found women learning to knit, sew and do other tasks that were traditionally viewed as the work of women – a far cry from Joice's role as a military commander. She explained that the majority of women inside the country had been deprived of education. They were eager to learn skills that could generate income for their families.

I interviewed a British mercenary soldier who had changed sides. He spoke freely about the brutal tactics that he had been taught and that were used against civilians inside Rhodesia. He seemed to have repented and also wanted to save his life. I wasn't completely convinced that he was genuine and warned the comrades that he might be a spy in their midst. They found that very funny and told me that he was never given that kind of access to their plans and activities but was kept as an 'honorary guest' in a safe house in Maputo.

Conducting interviews, raising funds, writing reports, helping out in the education office, visiting the camps and buying supplies in Swaziland filled my days with excitement and deepened my appreciation for my vocation. I had the freedom to pick up and leave my comfortable life in the States in exchange for being part of a cause for which many were ready to sacrifice their lives. I shared the hardships of daily living in a country under siege and the insecurity of not knowing if we would be bombed or attacked. I communicated by fax with the Zimbabwe Project Office in London that was run by Brother Arthur and Fr Scholz, my former companions in the Justice and Peace Commission. They in turn stayed in touch with the Maryknoll Sisters.

In a sense, I was cut off from the rest of the world but I never felt alone or afraid. I was surrounded by companions who welcomed me and who made me feel a part of their struggle. In Maputo I attended funerals for some of the comrades who died and discovered, as I mentioned earlier, that malaria was a bigger killer than enemy bullets. The funerals were very solemn affairs, with salutes, singing and words of appreciation. I was often moved to tears as I reflected on the lives cut short by illness, malnutrition or common tropical diseases. I was also moved to tears when I was taken to a house for those who had been injured in the war, losing limbs and being psychologically scarred as well.

In August 1979, I was told that a big surprise was waiting for me. I was taken to a local hotel where I met a group of Catholic Sisters from Sister Rocha's community and a Jesuit brother who had been kidnappèd from Marymount Mission in the north-east of the country and stayed with the guerrillas inside Mozambique for almost four months. I had heard about their capture from Brother Arthur and Fr Scholz who asked me to find out if they were safe. When I asked, I was assured that they were being well cared for and that one day I would see them. One of them was Sr Irene Rufaro, whose case I had covered when I first joined the Justice and Peace Commission. Irene had been moved from Wedza (Hwedza) to Makonde where two German Jesuits, a priest and a brother, were murdered by guerrilla forces. She then moved to Marymount and was kidnapped. We joked that she was a lightning rod for disaster.

I was asked to entertain the group and took them to FASCIM, the annual trade fair that was held in Maputo. We were like little children looking at the various exhibitions and buying ice cream cones. They told me about their experiences in various military camps where they had been held and assured me that they were treated with kindness and respect and were encouraged to pray. I told them about the needs in the refugee camps, trying to recruit them to stay and work with the refugees. Vice President Muzenda had often talked about his wish to have priests and sisters present in the camps to minister to the needs of the refugees. He had spoken to the Papal Nuncio about it and it seemed that there was no objection in principle to this request. In practice, however, religious communities that operated inside Rhodesia had heard so many chilling stories about the liberation forces that none were prepared to release any of their members to this mission. They had been told that they would be forbidden to wear their habits or to pray and would be forced to adopt Marxism. I believed that there was an opportunity to convince these sisters to stay. They seemed open to the idea but we should have known that it would never happen. Apparently, the Archbishop of Salisbury, Patrick Chakaipa, under pressure from the families of the sisters and their religious superiors, ordered them to return home. The sisters assured me that they would ask their superiors to let them return to work in the camps. This never happened either but it paved the way for sisters to live and work in camps of Mozambican refugees inside Zimbabwe after the war was over.

The following day a press conference was held in Maputo to present the sisters and brother to the media as well as two other prisoners that had been held by ZANU, a white farmer and the wife of another white farmer. General Tongogara chaired the briefing that was attended by all the press corps in Maputo. Sister Irene spoke for the Marymount contingent, stressing how well they had been looked after. The other prisoners said the same, with the woman telling how she was carried in a wheelbarrow since her legs were swollen and made it difficult to walk long distances. It was a huge propaganda coup for ZANU. Coming a few weeks before the leaders were to depart for the Lancaster House Conference, it gave them a head start in winning over public opinion.

After the press conference, Sr Irene, General Tongogara and I went outside and chatted on the lawn. He had been very impressed by the Sisters and their commitment to their vocation. 'If we had a dozen fighters like these sisters, we could easily have won the war by now', he joked. He admired the way the Sisters and Brother Herman had adapted to the tough life in the bush. Tongo then teased Irene that the next time that they met he might not be so kind and helpful. She teased back, saying that the next time they met she might not be so obliging either. We all went away in good humor as the Sisters prepared to depart for Rhodesia and General Tongogara got ready to attend the conference in London.

13

The Diplomatic Front: Lancaster House

The various Catholic aid agencies that were assisting Zimbabwean refugees in Mozambique and Zambia through the Zimbabwe Project came together annually to compare notes and determine priorities for the coming year. Dieter Scholz and Arthur Dupuis, who were deported and were now in the London office, sent a telex message, inviting me to come to London for the annual CIDSE meeting in 1979. The timing was perfect, since it coincided with the diplomatic initiative to bring together all parties to negotiate an end to the war in Rhodesia.

The diplomatic mission of David Owen, the British Foreign Secretary, and Andrew Young, the US ambassador to the United Nations, to persuade the liberation movements to attend an all-party conference to be held in London had been successful. ZANU and ZAPU agreed to come under the banner of the Patriotic Front and the Rhodesian Front government of Ian Smith also accepted to attend. The CCJP in Rhodesia had long advocated for such a gathering to bring all the warring parties together to find a negotiated settlement to end the conflict that was becoming more costly and brutal each month.

Hopes were high as the respective delegations arrived in London. ZANU, under the leadership of Robert Mugabe, chose to live in houses around the city while the ZAPU delegation, led by Joshua Nkomo, stayed in a hotel. Fr Michael Traber, who had first introduced me to the liberation struggle and who was instrumental in establishing the Zimbabwe Project and getting me assigned as its representative in Mozambique, was working in London at the time with the World Association for Christian Communication, an ecumenical venture that offered training to media practitioners from around the world. I stayed in his basement flat in a suburb of London, travelling each day by underground to the Zimbabwe Project offices located in the CIIR building in Regents Park.

Mike and I had the unique privilege of being invited to dine with some of the delegates that we knew from ZANU on many occasions. Fortunately, most of those we knew were staying together in the same house – General Tongogara, Vice President Simon Muzenda, Political Commissar Josiah Tungamirai, Head of Security, Emmerson Mnangagwa, and Education Secretary Dzingai Mutumbuka. The evenings that we spent with them gave us a rare glimpse into the discussions taking place at the Lancaster House Conference as well as the feelings and attitudes of some of the key players in the talks.

The first time we were invited, Mike brought portable short-wave radios for Comrades Tongogara and Tungamirai. I watched in fascination at the ritual that took place for receiving gifts within the liberation movement. Josiah Tungamirai saluted Tongogara and asked permission to keep the radio. I almost laughed aloud since it was so similar to the ritual that we Maryknoll Sisters followed when we were given a gift. We too had to ask our superiors for permission to accept a gift. After the exchange of gifts, both military leaders expressed deep concern at the daily reports that they were receiving from the front of bombing along the border areas, killing many of the new recruits who had been infiltrated into the country. 'I cannot send more young people to be killed', lamented General Tongogara, 'We must end this war'.

Tongogara's presence at Lancaster House was an eye-opener to the other delegations and to the British and American officials who were leading the process. He was known only by his reputation directing operations in Rhodesia and his occasional travels to friendly countries like China to plead for more weapons and funds. He was a shadowy figure around whom many rumors circulated. He totally disarmed Ian Smith when he greeted him on the opening day, asking about his mother and telling Smith that she used to give him sweets as a boy. He wooed the media as well with his captivating smile and ability to respond to questions with humor and clarity in impeccable English. The two political leaders, Robert Mugabe and Joshua Nkomo, paled in comparison with this flamboyant and charismatic military leader about whom little was known. He laughed at his own expense, enjoying the spectacle of men in suits, expecting him to be dressed in military fatigues and unable to communicate in English.

One evening, Tongogara showed me a cartoon published in a right-wing South African magazine by a Christian group. It showed a nun in a long habit and a devil with a pitchfork and a tail. The caption read, 'Sister Janice shaking hands with the devil'. We had a good laugh when he pointed to the devil, 'I recognize myself but this nun doesn't look like you'.

That evening and on many other occasions, he and Josiah Tungamirai shared their own close calls with death. They both had chilling stories of narrowly escaping being caught and killed. Tongo told of hiding in a drain pipe while Rhodesian forces searched the area, walking back and forth over the pipe but never bending down to look inside it. Josiah Tungamirai told of leaving a rural shop and coming face to face with Rhodesian forces. He ran and hid behind a tree. The enemy failed to find him. Both men credited divine intervention for their survival. They were aware of the dangers of guerrilla warfare and did not take lightly the risks to which their forces were exposed. They were not hardened by war but remained deeply concerned about the men and women under their leadership. I was touched by their vulnerability and openness to share their deepest fears and concerns with us.

Another evening, Bishop Zwane from Swaziland dined with us at the ZANU residence. He was in London for a church conference and was eager to meet the liberation leaders. During the meal, Emmerson Mnangagwa told the story of how he and other security officers had followed two prisoners who had escaped from ZANU custody in Mozambique and fled to Swaziland. They were young recruits who were accused of joining a rebel group within ZANLA. 'We followed them to the bishop's residence', he said. To laughter around the table, he announced that he and his men decided it would not be good manners to invade the bishop's residence so they returned to Maputo empty-handed. Bishop Zwane responded that he gave asylum to any who asked for it, without demanding to be told why they were fleeing. 'They may be here in London now, as I put them on the plane myself', he informed Emmerson. Emmerson took this news calmly and half-jokingly replied that the next time he wouldn't fail to catch his quarry. Zwane shot back that the next time he would take better precautions so the escapees wouldn't be found. I kept quiet during this exchange as I had met the two escapees at the Zimbabwe Project office a few days previously, when they came to ask for assistance in going for further studies. Both young men wrote down their experience of being political prisoners and were helped by the Project.

I also was invited to join Robert Mugabe and his wife Sally for a meal at their London residence. When I arrived, Robert answered the door and took me upstairs to the bedroom where Sally was resting. He had collected some mail from the table downstairs and gently brushed the envelopes across Sally's forehead to wake her up. She opened her eyes and the two exchanged loving glances. 'I brought you a friend', he announced, as I stepped forward. Sally sat up, gave me a hug and invited me to help her prepare the evening meal. Together we chopped vegetables in the small kitchen and Sally prepared *sadza* and chicken. I don't remember what we talked about around the supper table in London that evening but I went away uplifted and encouraged by their intelligence, integrity and their obvious love and respect for one another.

When Robert was in prison, Sally had often stayed with Mildred Neville, head of CIIR, when she was in London. Mildred connected her to various groups to whom Sally gave talks and collected clothing and funds for the refugees. Sally had been a teacher in her native Ghana before she met and married Robert Mugabe, who was also teaching in Ghana. She had been raised a Protestant but in order to marry Robert, a practicing Catholic, she took lessons in the Catholic faith and joined the Church. She took her faith seriously, carrying out works of mercy for the poor and forgotten in her adopted country. She also took politics seriously and was active in protests against minority rule in Rhodesia and in mobilizing women to get involved.

When her husband was imprisoned, Sally did not return to Ghana, but continued to lobby for majority rule in Zimbabwe. She travelled to various European cities to win support for the struggle and found a receptive audience among the Catholic parishes that she addressed in London and other major cities. When I came to Maputo, she and Robert were living in a house not far from the ZANU offices. She was involved in the Women's Center in Matola, a suburb of Maputo, that ZANU had established to teach practical skills to the women who had joined the struggle and

Sally helped to raise funds for it.

Dzingai Mutumbuka put me to work in London, drafting funding proposals for the schools in the refugee camps in Mozambique. Since the outcome of the peace talks was uncertain, ZANU made plans for an extended stay outside the country. Dieter, Arthur and I continued to raise funds for the camps in both Zambia and Mozambique. Judith Todd, daughter of former Southern Rhodesia Prime Minister Garfield Todd and his wife Grace, was the project officer in Zambia, fulfilling much the same role that I played in Mozambique. After visiting the ZAPU leaders in Lusaka and the refugee camps, she wrote funding proposals to address the inmates' needs. One particular request – for condoms – caused debate within the Project. We did not see how we could ask Catholic agencies for this since the Church's position against artificial birth control was well known although not always observed. It was common knowledge that women were often violated during wars. Judith explained that the provision of condoms would give women some protection and control over their bodies and might save them from unwanted pregnancies and from contracting sexually transmitted diseases. The condoms were provided although I don't remember which agency gave the funds for this unusual but highly practical request.

As the Christmas holidays were coming nearer, the Lancaster House conference hit a hurdle over the issue of the land. I clearly recall that Comrades Tongogara and Tungamirai returned one evening very crestfallen. Tongogara proclaimed that the liberation movements and the people of Zimbabwe should not be forced to pay for the land as a condition for ending the war. 'We will return to the forest to fight', he declared. 'Even if there are only a handful of us, we will start the war all over again. We can't in conscience pay for land that was stolen from us'. Josiah Tungamirai concurred. The mood was gloomy all through the meal.

The following day we learned that a compromise had been reached. The British and American governments agreed to provide funds to buy land from white farmers. This impasse resolved, the issues of a ceasefire and transitional arrangements were quickly made and conference soon came to an end with all parties agreeing to the draft Constitution that had been the result of their deliberations. I left London full of hope for the future, returning to Maryknoll, New York, to brief our leadership and then on to Pittsburgh to spend the holidays with my parents. I was due to return to Mozambique in mid-January to continue my work with ZANU and the Zimbabwe Project. Full of joy, I had no hint of the dark clouds on the horizon or of the challenges that lay ahead.

14

Transition to an Independent Zimbabwe

I always enjoyed returning to the home in which I grew up in Pittsburgh where my parents would pamper me and I could relax and escape from all the pressures of living in another culture and being the odd one out. The day after Christmas, my mother, father and I were having supper when a phone call came for me. It was my old friend Mildred Neville calling from CIIR in London. 'I have some bad news', she said simply. 'Tongogara was killed in a car accident in Mozambique'. I cried out in disbelief and shock. I bombarded her for more information as the tears streamed down my cheeks. 'We only know that he was on his way to the camps to brief the ZANLA forces about the agreements made at Lancaster House', she said. 'Perhaps more details will come later. I wanted you to know before you heard it on the news'.

Still crying, I hung up and threw myself face down on my parents' bed, cursing and crying until I could cry no more. My father came into the room and told me that he knew how I must feel. His best friend had died a few months before and he was still grieving for him. He said I should stay there and cry for as long as I needed and not worry about eating or helping with the dishes. I was grateful for his understanding and surprised at his vulnerability.

Questions and thoughts chased each other in my head. I was sure that the ceasefire was doomed and that none of the guerrillas would go to the assembly points when they heard that their charismatic leader was dead. I began to suspect foul play since it seemed impossible that a genuine road accident could occur so soon after the delegations had returned from London. Tongogara has been so prominent at the talks that I wondered if there was jealousy and internal power struggles involved. Or maybe it was a double agent who wanted the peace agreement to fail and for ZANU to be defeated in another way since it had not lost on the battlefield? I was making myself sick with my doubts, suspicions and grief.

I decided that I needed to get in touch with Julius Nyerere, President of Tanzania, who had played such a critical role in supporting the liberation struggle and also in supporting the diplomatic initiative. Maryknoll had close links with him and I had met him several times so I felt that I had a duty to communicate with him and urge him to extend the period of the ceasefire and to call for an investigation into the 'accident'. I can't recall how I managed to send the message but I learned that it had reached him and that Mozambique was planning to conduct its own investigation into what happened on the road between Xai Xai and Chimoio, which took the life of this extraordinary man.

I was due to return to Maputo in the middle of January, 1980, and left the States as planned. When I arrived back, I found that my friends in ZANU were as devastated as I was. Each one told me exactly where they were and what they were doing when the news came through. It reminded me of the death of President John F.

Kennedy when anyone alive at that time, could recall exactly when and where they heard the news. I learned that a messenger had brought the news first to ZANU Vice President, Simon Muzenda who then conveyed it to President Mugabe and other senior leaders.

There was a heaviness and sadness in each comrade that I met. The exhilaration that had heralded the successful conclusion of the peace conference was totally overshadowed by the tragedy of this great loss. I felt a special bond with Angelina, Tongogara's widow who was expecting their fourth child, and the three boys who had hardly known their father and now would never have the chance to know the man who had sacrificed life with his family to liberate his country.

On weekends I was often asked to take Tongo's children to play by the sea. We swam in the warm water of the Indian Ocean and built castles in the sand while their mother stayed in the house mourning and preparing for the birth of another child. The baby was born in Holy Week and it was a resurrection experience for all of us in Maputo. The baby was a girl and was named *Nyaradzo* or Comforter. Abandoning her black mourning clothes, Angelina brought the baby to the various offices so we could see her and be lifted up by the new life that had been born. Never have I felt the joy of Easter as I did then, as we sang and welcomed this child that carried the hopes and dreams of Comrade Tongo to his immediate family and to his extended ZANU family as well.

I was not given time to mourn his death since ZANU had decided to keep the refugee schools in Mozambique in operation after Independence while the Party made arrangements to build new schools for them inside the country where they could continue the experiments begun in the camps in Mozambique and Zambia. Once more I travelled north to Matenje and marveled at the creativity and commitment of the teachers who worked with few books, on desks and benches made of bamboo by the students, and with a few pencils and exercise books that I brought back on my trips to Swaziland. The truck that I had bought was now bringing supplies to the camps, cases of malaria had been reduced due to the medication that was distributed each week and the soccer balls and other recreational supplies were a welcome change on the playing field from the balls made of plastic bags held together with string.

When I returned to Maputo I found a telex from Dieter and Arthur informing me that I should not attend the Independence celebrations in Salisbury, Rhodesia as the bishops felt it would be too controversial. I called London and tried to convince them, that this made little sense. I had been asked to accompany Tongogara's family to the celebration and would find it most embarrassing to explain that the bishops were opposed to my presence. I finally won them over and travelled with Tongogara's three children on the plane from Maputo to Salisbury and accompanied them to Rufaro Stadium on the night of 18 April 1980. Their mother had decided to stay behind in Maputo and to return home later with the body of her husband when he was to be buried.

Rufaro Stadium on the night of April 18 was full of excitement as people crowded in to be part of this historic moment. I was seated in a VIP section behind the platform where the ceremony would be held. Across the field, Bob Marley, the legendary singer from Jamaica, entertained the crowd with his reggae melodies that made us stand up and dance. As the crowds poured into the small stadium and climbed trees outside to get a better view, police fired teargas into those pushing to enter an already overcrowded venue. The acrid fumes reached the area where I was sitting and we all put handkerchiefs over our mouths while tears streamed down our cheeks. Bob Marley and his Wailers continued to play and entertain the crowd and soon the smoke blew away and we could once more breath freely.

The actual ceremony was brief and meaningful. Archbishop Patrick Chakaipa, head of the Catholic Church in the country, offered the opening prayer. Justice McDonald, a stalwart of the Rhodesian Front, administered the oath of office to Robert Mugabe, the incoming Prime Minister, while Ian Smith, his predecessor looked on. Prince Charles, representing the British Queen, was also on the small stage. All stood at attention as an eternal flame was lit and the Union Jack lowered and replaced by the new flag of independent Zimbabwe. There were no speeches or other formal activities. The highlight of the evening was the entrance of about a hundred freedom fighters dressed in their khaki uniforms, singing liberation songs and marching around the stadium. The crowd erupted into loud cheering and clapping as these young men and women danced and sang with great enthusiasm. These were the heroes of the struggle, the sons and daughters of the ordinary Zimbabweans who had sacrificed so much to gain their freedom. 'Beautiful Zimbabwe' rang out into the chilly night air as we all stood and joined in this moving song that symbolized the hopes and dreams of the people.

I attended Mass the following day at St Peter's Church in Mbare, one of the African townships that had been the home of many of the nationalist leaders and young freedom fighters. The Mass began with a long procession that wound through the township accompanied by popular hymns from which the freedom songs had been composed. Tim Sheehy, the Zimbabwean desk officer at CIIR, who had been the main contact for the Justice and Peace Commission throughout the war, was also there. He was married to a Zimbabwean, Mary Ann Acton, whose family was well known and respected and whose ancestor had once proclaimed the prophetic words, 'Power corrupts and absolute power corrupts absolutely.' During those heady first days of the new Zimbabwe, those words of warning were easily forgotten.

The few days that I remained in Harare were a whirlwind of invitations to events attended by the members of the new government. Once vilified as 'terrorists', they now were in great demand. I recall in particular, a luncheon at the Dominican Convent at Fourth Street, opposite the Justice and Peace Office from which I had been arrested. Dzingai Mutumbuka, who would be the Minister of Education in the new government, was guest of honor. Some of the Dominican Sisters had been deeply involved in supporting the liberation struggle and had known Dzingai or Barnabas, as he was known when he was a student at Gokomere Mission in Gutu and then at the University of Southern Rhodesia or the University of Zimbabwe, as it's now known, and was active in Catholic clubs.

Soon it was time for me to take Tongogara's children back to their mother in Maputo and to resume my work with the Zimbabwe Project. There was no fallout from the bishops about my presence and I doubt if they even knew that I had been there. I realized, however, that many suspicions and doubts about the new government that was labeled 'Marxist' were still to be overcome. The Catholic Church, with its negative experience of communism in Eastern Europe, was especially cautious in its dealings with the new leaders, even though many were Catholics and known personally in their respective dioceses.

15

Strengthening Links with Mozambique

Back in Maputo, I continued to visit the camps to see what was needed and would then travel to Swaziland to buy the critical supplies after the Zimbabwe Project raised the funds. ZANU, as mentioned above, had decided to keep the children in the refugee schools in Mozambique until they were able to prepare adequately for their return. A plan had been made within the Education Department of ZANU to build on the experience of the schools in the struggle and to keep the children and their teachers together to create a new model of education in Zimbabwe. Fay Chung was given the task of locating farms inside Zimbabwe on which to build the schools since the idea was to be self-sufficient in food production and to develop a curriculum that was better suited to Zimbabwe's rural economy than the academic British one that they had inherited.

I would later be deeply involved in setting up these schools but in the early months after Independence, Minister Mutumbuka gave me a new assignment. I was tasked with a team of former freedom fighters to establish a 'School of Administration and Ideology' in

Maputo that was intended to train some of the older students who had completed secondary school to take up secretarial and administrative positions when they returned home. The leadership realized that there was a need for trained personnel who shared the ideals of the liberation struggle at every level of government. They were aware that many of the former civil servants would try to sabotage any efforts to bring change. It was urgent, therefore, to prepare a new and ideologically committed group of new recruits who could take over certain middle-level positions in government and staff the new ministries and offices that were being set up throughout the country to promote rural development.

Dennis Mavhiya, one of ZANU's officers, was my partner in bringing this new vision to life. We were given a team of teachers who had joined the struggle from various universities. Morris Mtsambiwa and Mike Fungati, had been students at Roma University in Lesotho. Augustine Mpofu had been a student at St Augustine's in Penhalonga, near the border with Mozambique. He was among those who had been rounded up and imprisoned by ZANU during the war due to internal divisions within the liberation movement and was released when the war came to an end. Cde Ropa represented ZANU's Education Department on the planning committee for this venture. Fox Gava (General Zvinavashe) was the senior ZANLA commander who was in charge of the troops that remained within Mozambique. This included the comrades who had lost limbs during the war and who were being fitted with prosthesis and given physical therapy. Cde Gava had helped to recruit the students for this experimental school. They were a mix of young men and women who were very bright and eager to learn.

They were also teen-agers who had been living in the bush with no outlets for their emotions and a normal desire to have fun. Discipline, therefore, soon became an issue. The teachers and I grappled with how to guide twenty impressionable young people without resorting to coercion or physical force. I recall one meeting that went long into the night where we brainstormed other methods for instilling discipline and punishing wrongdoing. We rejected using manual labor as a punishment since we wanted to instill in them an understanding that working with one's hands was noble and not to be scorned. This was a huge challenge since the colonial culture had relegated the black population to manual jobs, reserving the management positions for whites only. We considered using isolation as a form of punishment since a sense of community was such a strong element of the culture. In the end, we rarely had to use any of these, since both students and teachers were highly motivated and did not openly rebel or disobey.

There was one highly embarrassing incident, however, that proved that we had underestimated the problem. The senior commander, Fox Gava, was coming to Maputo from the military camps in the north and we were asked to prepare an entertainment for him. The students practiced poems, dances and a short play to present at a celebratory meal. I was looking forward to the evening and had no doubt that it would be a success. Unfortunately, beer was served and by the time the entertainment began, some of the students were drunk and were not able to properly remember or say their lines. One of them was the MC whose antics made me want to hide under the table.

Cde Gava called a halt to this chaotic scene. He scolded the staff and students and told them that he would return in a week and expected a totally different performance. He then took me aside and gave me a dressing down that I will always remember and appreciate. 'Sister Janice, we brought you here because we trusted you and we thought that you would lead by example and show these young people how to behave. You have let us down. You need to be strict; to let them know what is right and what is wrong. They have been in the bush under military discipline. You have to teach them another model of self-respect and respect for others. You know, they are not allowed to drink or to go out on dates. What if one of the girls gets pregnant? What are you doing to prepare them to lead others when they go home'? He continued in like manner for quite some time. I could not ignore his message. When we rejoined the group, he repeated his request that I take a leadership role. Again, I tried to decline and was voted down by the staff and students. As a missioner, I had been taught to take a back seat and to groom local people to take leadership positions and to hand over to them. Now I was being asked to step forward to the front. It felt awkward at first but gradually I assumed more responsibility.

I looked up to Commander Gava and accepted his request since he was held in great respect and a certain amount of fear. We always knew when he was in Maputo because the whole atmosphere changed when he was around. All the officers in every department went about their duties with more vigor and commitment. There were few delays and no excuses when things went wrong. I watched and saw how Cde Gava led by example and by his words of encouragement as well as criticism. He was straightforward and fair. This was the highest compliment that could be given. 'He is strict but he is very fair', I heard said about him. I experienced it myself and agreed with this description of his particular gift of leadership.

Cde Gava showed his leadership skills in another way by setting up a committee of all the ZANU departments to determine the needs in the camps. I no longer had to go from office to office, waiting for hours and even days to see someone who would give me information. Now I met weekly with all the department heads or their deputies and received firsthand reports that I could write up and send to London in order to raise funds for the particular needs. I was privileged to have this insider access to many of the leaders of ZANU and I came to the meetings well prepared with questions and an idea of what the donors overseas would be willing to fund and what was off limits. I knew that anything that seemed even faintly related to the military would not be accepted. This was often a disappointment to the leaders but they came to understand and were realistic in their requests. I was impressed by their knowledge of their respective departments and their concern for those under their care.

In planning for the School of Administration and Ideology, Dennis Mavhiya and I decided that it should be closely linked to our Mozambican counterparts and that the curriculum should utilize some of the most successful projects in Mozambique such as cooperatives, communal villages, schools and community development projects We, therefore, met with various leaders in FRELIMO and arranged for the students to go on field trips to these projects that were located throughout Maputo. In addition to conducting research and writing about these initiatives, we thought that students could also be attached to them and get some in-service training in how such endeavors were managed.

Our contacts and guides for these exposure programs were two of the most highly respected academics in the country, Aquino de Braganca, head of the Centre for African Studies at Eduardo Mondlane University, Maputo, was an adviser to President Samora Machel, a journalist and anti-colonial activist in his native Goa and in the Portuguese colonies on the African continent. Aquino welcomed the idea of closer cooperation with ZANU and made the necessary contacts for us. Ruth First, his deputy, was equally enthusiastic. A well-known anti-apartheid activist in her native South Africa, she had been imprisoned there and was eventually forced into exile. They were visionary people with international experience Our meetings with them stretched me further intellectually and gave me a deep appreciation of the value of committed scholarship.

Aquino, as a confidante of President Machel, asked me to meet him on several occasions to talk about Zimbabwe's liberation struggle and the role of various leaders. He trusted me with his personal views and his concerns about the internal conflicts within the liberation movement. Aquino was very impressed by Tongogara, whom he had met many times since Tongo often visited the Centre for Africa Studies when he came to Maputo and would have stimulating discussions with the staff about the liberation struggle and what would be needed to transform society after Independence. Aquino said he admired General Tongogara's intelligence, sense of humor and his leadership qualities. He was very upset when Tongo died as he felt that he would have been able to create a revolutionary army and to influence other aspects of the old colonial society.

Whenever we spoke, Aquino took me driving along Costa da Sol, as he did not want others to overhear the conversation. He told me that when there were internal struggles within ZANU, he advised President Samora Machel to trust Tongo. Aquino died in the plane crash that took the life of President Machel and 33 others in October 1986. Lured off its course by a beacon set up by apartheid South Africa, the plane crashed into a mountain, killing all passengers on board.

Ruth First was killed by a letter bomb delivered to her at the Institute in 1982. The wife of Joe Slovo, senior member of the African National Congress (ANC) and head of the South African Communist Party, Ruth was a renowned scholar and activist in her own right. Her death and that of Aquino robbed not only Mozambique, but southern Africa and the world of two people who could have helped steer the new nations of Zimbabwe, Mozambique and South Africa with their international experience and scholarship and their whole-hearted commitment to revolutionary change.

While their deaths would come much later, long after I had left Mozambique, I was reminded of the deaths of thousands of young people in the refugee camps that had happened a few years before. The occasion was one of the programs that we had set up with the Mozambique Film Institute, then headed by Polly Gaster, a *cooperante* from England who had arrived shortly after Mozambique gained Independence and was active in promoting Mozambique internationally. She had arranged a screening of two films made by Mozambican film-makers in the aftermath of the raid on two camps of Zimbabweans by Rhodesian forces – Nyadzonia in 1976 and Chimoio in 1977. In the case of Nyadzonia, Rhodesian troops came to the camp disguised as Frelimo soldiers. Led by a deserter called Nyathi, they entered into the heart of the camp shouting FRELIMO slogans, opening fire on the unsuspecting youth who had assembled for the morning parade.

An estimated 1,028 were murdered that day, their bodies shoveled into a mass grave by FRELIMO troops who were called to the scene after the massacre. The film shows the lifeless bodies piled on top of each other in great disarray. A moving interview with a survivor, Ann Tekere, who hid in a pit latrine, described what happened. Ann could barely speak from the shock of what had taken place. A visibly distraught Josiah Tongogara, who had arrived at the scene not long after the Mozambican forces, tried to comfort her. Sweat and tears mingled as they viewed the carnage all around them.

There was complete silence in the theatre when the lights went on at the end of the film. Then one of the students started singing a moving refrain known by all: '*Ndeapi magamba*... Who are the heroes that we salute? They are those who died at Chimoio. Those who died at Nyadzonia. They are Nehanda, Takawira,

Tongogara...' The litany of those who gave their lives for the liberation of their country went on. Singing this mournful refrain, the students and staff processed out of the theatre into the night air, shaken by what they had seen. Some had been survivors of this attack and were inconsolable as they recognized some of the bodies on the ground and in the mass grave. Because they had escaped, they had not seen the utter devastation and horror that had taken place.

One of the students came over to me in the darkness and began to tell me his story. He told how he had joined the struggle as a student from secondary school with high ideas. He thought that his life would improve. Instead, he said that he lost everything. His clothes were in rags, his shoes were missing, he had no soap to bath himself. 'I began to wonder if I had made a mistake', he said. 'Then in my downtrodden position, I realized that my suffering was for the people'. His face lit up as he recalled this moment when his motivation was transformed. 'Now I live for the people', he said with conviction. 'Everything that I do is for the people. I will never betray them'. Valentine Mazorodze eventually wrote a novel about his wartime experiences. Called *Silent Journey from the East*, it depicts the hardships of the struggle as well as its ideals.

Our modest experiment in education attempted a few revolutionary changes. There was no official head, for instance, as we believed in a democratic system where instructors and students together worked out the rules and the structures that would guide this fledgling institution. We also tried to instill an appreciation of manual labor by requiring the students and staff to clean their own quarters, cook their food and grow food in a garden located at one of the hostels. We believed that working together would also prevent class divisions that have a tendency to arise in most institutions. No one was receiving a salary since the teachers were still soldiers employed by ZANU. The Party, therefore, supplied the food and other necessities.

I taught some classes in communication and filled in occasionally when one of the teachers was missing. The experiment was very exciting and was moving forward as planned. We felt that our idealism was not misplaced and that a school like this one could be self-governing The bonds among the staff were growing stronger day by day as we discussed and agreed on each and every aspect of this model project. The twenty-two students also seemed to be getting along without the usual tension between the men and the women

Just when we were congratulating ourselves and feeling that we were succeeding in our vision of a new school for a new society, we were shocked to be told that Edgar Tekere, the Minister of Manpower Planning in the newly elected government, had ordered the school to be closed. We tried to reach people who might explain why and prevent it from happening – Dzingai Mutumbuka, now Minister of Education in the new government, Simon Muzenda, now the Deputy Prime Minister, Fox Gava, the local commander, out of reach in the north of the country. We couldn't reach any of them, that might have saved this educational experiment. Witness Mangwende, who was the person in charge in the absence of Cde Gava, forced us to follow the orders that came from Minister Tekere in Harare. The students and teachers were flown to Harare in July 1980 and were disbanded. A few were given junior positions in the new government or the army and some were sent for further education but most were left to fend for themselves. By now I had flown to London to report to the Zimbabwe Project on the funding that we had received. I had planned to return to Maputo after the meeting but now everything was in disarray and there was little reason to go back.

When I arrived in London at the flat of Mildred Neville where I would be staying, I was met at the door by more bad news Mildred told me that our friend and supporter, Bishop Zwane, had died in Swaziland – also in a car accident, not unlike that of Tongogara. He had recently spoken out in favor of sanctions against South Africa at a meeting of all the bishops of southern Africa. Could this 'accident' have been arranged by South African special forces, who thought nothing of invading neighboring countries and killing people suspected of supporting the ANC? I had been with him only three weeks before his death, buying more supplies for the refugee camps and staying at his house in Manzini. I recalled our last conversation when he told me that I probably should not work in Zimbabwe after Independence. 'You will have to speak out about the injustices of the new government just as you spoke out against the colonial government of Ian Smith', he said, warning me not to expect that the new rulers of the country would be saintly and incorruptible. He reminded me of the men and women that ZANU had imprisoned within its own ranks, two of whom he had helped to escape. He did not romanticize the struggle but had a realistic view of human beings, knowing that they could be heroic and make sacrifices at times and then be selfish, cruel and corrupt at other times. 'We all need redemption', he reminded me, 'Not once, but over and over again'. His words rang true at this difficult moment when, what we had worked to achieve in Maputo had been undone and when my own future was uncertain.

16

Opposing Visions of the Church

From the first moment that I set foot in Mozambique in 1978, I was bombarded with questions about religion and revolution. Zimbabweans and Mozambicans alike, as well as expatriate missionaries and journalists, seemed to be fascinated by the topic. They queried whether Christianity was compatible with a socialist revolution and whether the Catholic Church in particular could support an armed struggle. I was seen as an exception. I also posed this same question to the leaders of ZANU and FRELIMO that I met. Some of these appeared in print and reveal the differences between the history of Mozambique and Zimbabwe.

The night of my arrival in Mozambique, a year after I had been deported from Rhodesia, Simon Muzenda, the Vice-President of ZANU and a Catholic from Gweru Diocese, came to welcome me at the apartment of Roberta Washington, an architect from New York who was volunteering her services in the newly independent country. I had heard about Cde Muzenda from Fr Mike Traber and knew that he had been a leader in the church in Gweru and that his wife and children remained in Rhodesia and were being given financial assistance by the Bethlehem Fathers.

On this evening, as mentioned previously, he had come with Tendi Ndlovu, one of the students who had been abducted from St Albert's Mission in the north-east of the country in 1974. He wanted me to hear her story and to know that there were good Catholics in the struggle. Over the months that I was in Maputo, I grew to admire Simon Muzenda and to witness how he put his faith into action. For instance, he enabled a branch of Caritas, the international Catholic confederation of 165 relief, development and social service organisations operating in 200 countries, to be established in Mozambique against the objections of FRELIMO and with reservations from the Catholic bishops of Mozambique, who were in a tenuous position in regard to the new government. His persistence and common-sense arguments finally prevailed. Not only was a Caritas office set up within the Catholic headquarters in Maputo but it became a lifeline for bringing supplies to refugees from Rhodesia and later to displaced persons in Mozambique.

Muzenda told me of a frustrating visit that he had with the Papal Nuncio in Maputo who set conditions for having priests and sisters in the camps of refugees. Apparently, the Nuncio made it clear that the priests should be allowed to say daily Mass in the camps and that the sisters should live in convents nearby but not in the camps. Even as he told me the story, his anger showed. 'I told him that the Church should not be the overseer but the demonstrator', he said. He went on to state that he told the Nuncio that priests and sisters 'can join us not as special people apart but as the same as us'. He apparently told the Nuncio that they should go for military training and face the same hardships as everyone else. 'The Church should learn from history', he explained to me, citing the mistakes of the Reformation and other times when the Church refused to change. Turning to the problem of the Church in Mozambique, he said, 'The Church here is static. It criticizes the government instead of criticizing itself'. He went on to proclaim: 'Africans will never be atheists. They will believe in God but may reject the Church'.[1]

I had a long conversation with Robert Mugabe about ZANU's attitude towards religion during my first visit to Mozambique. He allowed me to tape our conversation, which was eventually published by Mambo Press in a book of his speeches. He was very open and articulate, comparing the lives of the early Christians in the Acts of the Apostles to the kind of socialism that ZANU had adopted. 'We share the little that we have in common', he told me.

My former student at the AACC Training Center in Nairobi, Kenya, Bishop Zwane had become my teacher. His vision of a new church of the people excited me but I did not see how it could be achieved, given the hierarchical structure of the Catholic Church and its conservative stand on many issues. True, a few radicals like him were among the hierarchy; true, the conclusions of the Second Vatican Council offered a new theology and ecclesiology that could liberate the church from its old attitudes and structures. Mandla Zwane fully believed that a revolution was needed within the church just as much as a revolution was required in racist South Africa and minority-controlled Rhodesia.

'My fear is that the church will not be in a position to minister in a revolutionary situation', he wrote in an article for a publication called Black Christians and the Church in South Africa. 'It is because of our attitudes, because of our historical background, because of all kinds of things that have happened to us. We are imprisoned. We can only see things in terms of reformation. We only want to reform things, not radically change them. None of us is prepared for radical change. That is my fear'. He died before he was able to refute or confirm this rather depressing prediction.

His words, however, were being debated throughout the

---

1   McLaughlin, Janice, diary entry for 15 August 1979.

region. I spent long hours in stimulating discussions with priests in Mozambique who had supported FRELIMO's war of liberation. Now that freedom had come, they felt rejected by both sides – the Church saw them as traitors who had sided with Marxists who seized church property on coming into power, while FRELIMO, with its anti-Christian form of Marxism, did not fully accept them either. They were marginalized and felt betrayed.

I met with other Christian leaders who did not have the same dilemma as the Catholic priests. The head of the Christian Council, for instance, told me that the problem with the Catholic Church was the former Concordat between the Vatican and the Portuguese Government that had given privileges to the priests and bishops in the Portuguese colonies. 'I feel pity for the Catholic church', he said. 'They still have problems ahead. There is too much anti-communism. This is European thinking that is led by Italian priests'. He explained that recently the Catholics were the only church that refused to attend the Christian Peace Conference, although all churches had been invited to send delegates. 'This is an insult to the rest of us', he said, 'and it makes the government suspicious'.

Shavadin Khan, a member of FRELIMO, who had been given the role of helping to educate the bishops to accept change, shared his experiences with me. 'They feel guilty about the past', he said, referring to the Concordat, 'but they shouldn't. It wasn't their decision' In 1974, he took the Catholic bishops of Maputo and Beira to Tanzania to meet the bishops there. 'It opened their eyes, but they didn't keep up the exchange', he said.

I had learned about the Vatican Concordat with Portugal from some priests in Mozambique who had denounced it and were expelled. I wrote about this for the Kenyan press and helped to draft a similar statement for our Maryknoll community in East Africa. Adrian Hastings, a former member of the Missionaries of

Africa, better known as the White Fathers, published both of these statements in a book that explored the relationship between the Catholic Church and revolutionary movements.

Not all the hierarchy in Mozambique supported the Concordat. Bishop Pinto of Nampula Diocese, for example, was one of the exceptions. He spoke out against the relationship that tied the Catholic Church to the colonial power and made friends with the guerrilla forces of FRELIMO, The White Fathers in Mozambique renounced the Concordat in 1976 and were expelled for this stand. Josef Pampalk, who later left the priesthood and married my friend, Mary Salat, was one of them.

Kahn told me that during the liberation war, FRELIMO soldiers in Cabo Delgado built churches and selected people from the community to serve as leaders of prayer. When the Portuguese army destroyed these churches, the soldiers told him, 'Don't worry, we will build another. God is everywhere. He can't be destroyed'. These poignant stories spoke to me of lost opportunities for rapport between FRELIMO and the Catholic Church.

Khan said that Samora Machel met with some of the Church leaders and said to them: 'Look at our society. All races are living together; we are trying to create equal opportunities and sharing of resources. It's not much different from what you do'. After this meeting, President Machel asked Khan to talk to them and help educate them, 'you understand them and won't offend them, he said.[2]

Unfortunately, the relationship between Church and State deteriorated as the FRELIMO government seized almost all church property, including schools and clinics that had served the poor. President Machel became more critical in his public pronouncements. I attended a public rally outside the Catholic Cathedral in Maputo in March 1980 where Samora spoke for

---

2   McLaughlin, Janice, Diary entry for 5 March 1980, meeting with S. Kahn.

five hours. He entertained the crowds with song in between his long speech but I was hot, hungry and thirsty by the end of this marathon. I could not follow all his Portuguese but I picked up some of the main points. He mentioned, for instance, that the Pope would be coming to Mozambique. 'Let him come and go', he said, 'the Church we recognize is the priests and sisters who stayed and suffered with us. The Pope means nothing to us'.

I copied, from *Tempo* magazine, a particularly scathing speech that Machel gave in Beira in January 1980 where he castigated the priests and bishops for being on the side of the Portuguese and for continuing to have a foreign mentality. 'It was not them who conquered/gained independence', he declared, 'They had kept themselves at the side of colonialism until the end. They were blacks with Mozambican nationality but with a mentality of little Portuguese. None of them came to help us to liberate the people.... Before they are priests, bishops or archbishops, they have first to be Mozambicans; they have to defend the Mozambique nation and not join the enemy'.

This angry attack seemed to be the result of some documents that had been found in Beira that were critical of the government. 'It is starting from Beira that they spread insults against the People's Republic of Mozambique; it is from Beira that they spread their anti-patriotism... their fidelity to Portuguese education...., it is from there that documents emerge which prove how they miss colonial times, documents which prove how their mentality is enslaved to the foreign, which spread their lack of personality and patriotic pride, ...documents which show clearly the spirit of servitude'. He went on to condemn the position of the church during the colonial era; 'They were on the side of the colonial army as chaplains, received stripes and decorations, accepted the uniform which symbolized the crime. They abandoned the war zones and handed their chapels to become barracks of the colonial army where it massacred the people'.[3]

This kind of tirade produced much defensiveness among church personnel. I met the Apostolic Delegate in Maputo on 28 January, 1980, for one and a half hours during which he spoke mainly of the strained relations between church and state in the country. He told me that there were two priests in prison, both African. 'The bishops are true Mozambicans. They love their country. There was white power before. Now Africans are in leadership'. He pointed out that this had been a mistake and that he had advised Fr Randolph, the Secretary General of the Rhodesian Catholic Bishops' Conference, to advise Rome to make appointments of Africans to leadership positions before independence. He also defended the stand of most of the missionaries during the liberation war. 'We must distinguish: not all missionaries were colonial. Only the Portuguese', he said, stating that about 400 missionaries had opposed Portuguese colonial rule.[4]

When I stayed in Maputo with Mary Salat, I met her husband, Josef Pampalk, who drafted the statement against the Vatican. I was introduced to many of their priest friends who had taken a stand with the people during the war and continued to work for change in the church as well as in society. I spent hours debating with them and learning from them about the role of the church in a socialist society. Julio, a priest from Spain, told me that the bishops were becoming more reactionary. 'The Church wants power, it wants to control', he said. 'While the Party (FRELIMO) is beginning to accept that Christians can also be revolutionary, the Church hierarchy has a problem accepting this. It is withdrawing into pastoral programs and won't allow priests and sisters to work in communal villages because it says they are oppressive', Julio was very disappointed in what he had observed. He felt that the

---

3   Ibid., 28 January 1980, 'A Slave Mentality Toward the Foreign,' *Tempo*, January 27, 1980, No. 485, p. 25.
4   Ibid., 28 January 1980.

Church was separating Christians from others and from their task in the world. In spite of his pessimism, Julio remained committed to working with the people and trying to transform the church from within.[5]

These discussions stimulated me to deeper reflection on the role of the Church and missionaries like myself. Not long after my meeting with Julio, I wrote in my diary: 'I realize that I tend to interpret everything through a religious spectrum. I see the similarities between ZANU and Maryknoll when perhaps I should see the differences'. I posed some questions for reflection: 'Does a revolutionary party fulfill many of the same objectives as a religious community, only more effectively? Can some policies, structures, life-style, leadership of a Party be transferred to a religious organization and vice-versa? Is the Church in fact a kind of international super-Party'?[6]

I was steeped in liberation theology and the documents of Vatican II but I was not aware of feminist theology at that time. I was deeply critical, however, of a church that seemed to be out of touch with the ordinary person and that was dominated by men Clericalism was not part of my vocabulary then but I resented an all-male establishment that treated women as second-class citizens and took for granted our subservience. Ever the rebel, I became increasingly disillusioned with this structure. While I worked to promote participation in the ZANU School of Administration and Ideology, I felt powerless to change the structure of the Catholic Church.

Patriarchy was not a familiar concept to me although I was aware of cultural practices in Kenya, Zimbabwe and Mozambique that oppressed and exploited women. I was dismayed at the cases of domestic violence that I encountered as well as the unfaithfulness of most of the husbands of my female friends. It seemed that the

5   Ibid., 11 February 1980.
6   Ibid., 13 February 1980.

Church was no exception. Women were meant to cook, clean and arrange the flowers. Never were they permitted to take leadership roles or to speak their views in public. While this bothered me, I never considered walking away or abandoning my faith. If anything, my faith grew stronger as I encountered the resilience of women and their good humor in the face of such gross injustice. I also felt that my vocation gave me a certain freedom that was not readily available to married women with children. I could travel to war zones and take risks as no one depended on me for care and support. I also experienced respect from the people with whom I worked, including battle-hardened guerrillas. I used to tease them that I was treated like an 'honorary man'.

Myra Walters and Constantine Leonard Schaub, Sister Janice's
grandparents on her mother's side.

Patrick Francis
McLaughlin and
Mary Connelly,
Sister Janice's
grandparents on her
father's side.

1

Sr Janice aged
six months
with Katherine
Walters, 1942

Mary Ellen McLaughlin and Sr Janice c. 1946

2

Sr Janice and her sister Mary Ellen on holiday

Sister Janice

3

Mary Ellen and Sr Janice at JFK airport after her deportation from
Rhodesia in 1977
(Photo: DE LUCIA)

Sr Janice with her sister and her mother, 1993

Sr Janice with the Communication Coordinator of the church in
Nairobi, Kenya c. 1977
(Photo by Fr Morgan Vittengl, MM)

Sister Janice, President Julius Nyerere and Sister Jean Pruitt
Photo by Tanzania Information Services, official photographer

Casa Banana, Gorongosa, Mozambique

6

Fay King Chung teaching students at Matenje Camp in Mozambique

Students studying at Matenje Camp in Mozambique

7

Fungai Mahamba and Chipo Chung, Sister Janice's godchild

Students outside Sister Janice's home at Matenje Camp in
Mozambique where she lived fron 1977-1979

8

Sr Janice receiving the Martin Luther King Freedom Award, 1977
(Photo by Joseph Vail)

Sr Janice receiving the Black Catholic Ministries Award, Pittsburg,
Pennsylvania, 1978

Refugee students from the camps who would be placed at a ZIMFEP
school in early 1980

John Conradie and Fay King Chung

KgoKgo Mudenge, ZIMFEP Director, Sister Janice and Grace Todd c. 1980

Sr Janice, Fay King Chung, Headmaster Nyengera and Zimfep staff c. 1983

Sr Janice with the children of the late commander, Josiah Tongogara

Fr Fedelis Mukonori, Sr Janice, and George Houser,
1979

Sr Janice, Chipo Chung, her god-daughter, and Fay Chung, and, 1983
(Photo by Simon Muzenda)

Sr Janice, President Canaan Banana, Father Paul Newpower, 1982

The launch of the Zimbabwe Mozambique Friendship Society: Mike
Nasinigano with Sister Janice
(Photo by Sr. Jeri Stokes, MM)

Sr Janice always had a particular love of children/ Silveira House 2001
(Photo by Sr Bernice Kita, MM)

A sewing project at Silveira House, 2001
(Photo by Sr. Bernice Kita, MM)

Sr Chiyoung Pak, Sr Janice McLaughlin, Sr Patty Startup
Sr Jeong Mi Lee

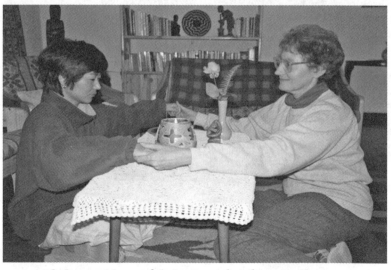

Sr Jeongmi Lee and Sr Janice at their home in Harare.

Sr Janice and Father Brian McGarry at the launch of
Conscience be my Guide, 2005.
(Photo. Weaver Press)

Murray McCartney and Sr Janice, Weaver Press, 2008

Sr Janice with Alice and Ranga Zinyemba at the launch of *In Pursuit of Freedom and Justice*, Harare, 2015.
(Photo by Cynthia Matonhodze. Weaver Press archive.)

Sr Janice with Rugare Gumbo at the launch of *In Pursuit of Freedom and Justice*, Harare, 2015.
(Photo by Cynthia Matonhodze. Weaver Press archive.)

Judi and Kathy Stewart with Sr Janice, Cape Town 2019
(Photo by Themba Stewart)

Maryknoll Congregational Leadership Team: Pictured from left to
right are Sr Rebecca Macugay (Vice President), Sr Janice McLaughlin
(President), Sr Bitrina Kirway (Team Member) and Sr Ann Hayden
(Team Member), 2019

Sr Janice and Mrs Dadirai Chikwekwete of AFCAST c. 2019
(Photo by Uchechukwu Oguike)

Sr Janice with Marlowe Chung, 2020
(Photo by Chipo Chung)

17

ZIMOFA:

Neighbors Helping One Another

I witnessed the huge price that Mozambique paid for its support of the liberation of Zimbabwe and South Africa when I was living and working there in 1979 and 1980. Roads and bridges were sabotaged by South African special forces and there was a blockade of goods coming from the south. As a result, there were shortages of food and other essential items. One could stand for hours in a queue for a loaf of bread while meat and vegetables were rare luxuries. I existed on a diet of avocado and grapefruit for weeks at a time and yearned for simply a glass of milk or a bowl of cereal.

In addition to the destruction of infrastructure by South African forces, the Rhodesian army carried out raids on camps of Zimbabwean exiles, be they military or civilian installations. I was also aware of a shadowy third force called RENAMO (Resistência Nacional Moçambicana), that had been set up in 1975 by the Rhodesians and South Africans to further undermine the independence of Mozambique. This force was composed largely of Mozambicans who did not agree with Frelimo's policies or were from regions that felt marginalized by the Frelimo government.

After it achieved Independence, Zimbabwe also experienced the effects of RENAMO, as it began to attack the pipeline that brought fuel from the port of Beira, Mozambique, to holding tanks in Mutare, Zimbabwe. In 1982, Zimbabwe sent troops to guard the pipeline. These forces along the Beira corridor were soon involved in protecting the civilian population as well, since people began to flock to the roadside to escape attacks on their villages. RENAMO was ruthless and kidnapped children to serve in its army and mutilated the people it did not kill by cutting off parts of their bodies, ears, noses, lips, hands and feet, as a sign to others to cooperate with RENAMO.

When I returned to independent Zimbabwe in 1981, I kept in touch with friends that I had made in Mozambique, many of them journalists who kept abreast of the destabilization being carried out against the country. The Zimbabwean media also carried reports on the death and destruction that was taking place in Mozambique and the role of the Zimbabwean army in that country. Journalists David Martin and Phyllis Johnson who had reported on Zimbabwe's liberation war, now turned their attention to documenting the destruction being carried out in the region. While the evidence was compelling, little was being done to stop the destabilization or to provide support to Mozambique.

As we had done many times before, Fay Chung and I put our heads together to see if there was anything that civilians like ourselves could do to assist the people of Mozambique. We knew that there was great appreciation for the assistance that Zimbabwe had received from Mozambique and that people could be motivated to help if provided with a way to do so. Fay and I met with the Mozambique Ambassador at the time and put forward the suggestion to him of forming an organization to mobilize support for the civilian population along the Beira corridor. Ambassador Manguni was enthusiastic about the idea and encouraged us to draw up a plan.

Fay and I brainstormed with others about establishing a Zimbabwe Mozambique Friendship Association and Mary Chimbodza (Gokova) came up with the name, ZIMOFA. We drew up a list of people to serve on the board, drafted a trust deed with the help of a lawyer and then met with Vice President Simon Muzenda who readily agreed to serve as patron of the organization. In no time we held our first public activity at Ranche House College in Harare. The principal of Ranche House at the time was Taka Mudariki, the former director of ZIMFEP, who gave us the premises free of charge and later opened the college to students from Mozambique sponsored by ZIMOFA.

We recruited several military people to serve on the board since we knew they were committed to help Mozambique, having benefitted from the generosity of Mozambique during the war. We also knew that we would need the support of the military to protect the convoy of goods that we collected and to make sure that they reached the displaced people. Colonel Clemence Gaza agreed to be the Chairperson and was very hands on, attending every event and travelling often to affected areas in Mozambique. Other board members included Air Marshall Josiah Tungamirai, Minister July Moyo, General Sheba Gava, David Popatlal, a businessman from Mozambique who had befriended ZANU during the war, Fay Chung and myself. We rented a house on the Avenues to serve as the office and hired Mike Nesangano, an ex-combatant to serve as project officer. The wife of the Canadian Ambassador, whose first name I remember, Teresa, volunteered to help raise funds and was a delightful companion on some of the trips that we made, to see for ourselves the extent of the need.

Francisco Madeira, the new Mozambican Ambassador to

Zimbabwe, was as enthusiastic as his predecessor and lent us Ignacio Palma, a Mozambican who proved invaluable in providing contacts and translating for us on our many trips inside the country. Palma was also skilled in getting us across borders quickly where the border personnel expected a 'favor'. He always carried enough packs of cigarettes and bars of soap to satisfy the guards who ushered us across with no questions asked. Soon the office was flooded with donations of food and clothing from ordinary Zimbabweans as well as large donations from local companies. We began sending truckloads of mealie meal across the border to feed the hungry people clustered along the Beira corridor. The army provided transport and helped to distribute the food.

We were told of camps of displaced people in Tête Province who had gathered at Chitima, a railway camp outside Tête. Air Marshall Tungamirai gave us a plane to fly there to see the situation for ourselves and to take needed food, blankets and other materials. Hundreds of people lay sleeping under railway cars and in tents.

The Zimbabwe army invited us to visit one of the largest gatherings of displaced people at one of its bases within Gorongosa Park. Called Casa Banana, it had been captured from RENAMO in 1985. The base held underground bunkers built for the Zimbabwean troops during the war and now used by Mozambique government troops. Thousands of internally displaced Mozambicans now lived in the camp in tents and make-shift houses. This trip was dangerous as RENAMO still had troops operating within Gorongosa, and it was heart breaking to see hundreds of starving people wearing a few tattered rags of clothing or none.

The pilot of the aircraft followed standard procedure in a war zone to avoid heat seeking missiles by flying high and then diving down for a landing. We seemed to be falling out of the sky when suddenly we swerved up again to avoid another plane that was taking off. We were seated on the floor hugging the sides of the plane and surrounded by the supplies that we had brought with us. The sudden descent followed by an equally sudden ascent had us holding our breath and our stomachs. If we had not been tied in place we would have been rolling around amid the bales of clothing and bags of mealie meal.

Climbing down from the plane on wobbly legs, we were met by hundreds of children waving and crying out a welcome to us. Sweat was soon dripping from every pore of my body as Gorongosa seemed to trap the hot humid air. I wondered if the underground bunkers provided some relief for the soldiers. We were invited to see for ourselves. They did provide relief from the heat and the insects but the misery of the local people who surrounded the base was impossible to escape.

Ignacio Palma accompanied me around the camp and translated as I met with women who had seen their husbands murdered before their eyes and their sons kidnapped to serve as RENAMO soldiers. They recounted these horrors with stoicism as their younger children clung to them. I wondered how they would ever recover from the trauma they had experienced. An older woman was cooking leaves from the trees and told me that was all that she had eaten for the past two weeks. The camp held mostly women and children and a few older men as the younger men had either been killed or kidnapped.

We thanked the Zimbabwean army for its mission of mercy, trying to save the lives of these desperate people. As we boarded the plane to return to Harare, each of us held back tears and sat in silence reflecting on what we had seen and heard. We were soon shaken out of our reverie as the plane ascended sharply and then skimmed the tree tops to avoid being shot down by RENAMO rockets.

Our work was getting positive publicity in the media and the donations flooded into the small office and were soon loaded on trucks and delivered to those in most need. We didn't want to portray only negative images of Mozambique and widened our mission to include cultural exchanges and educational initiatives. We brought the world acclaimed Mozambique National Dance Troupe to perform to a packed hall at the Sheraton Hotel and we brought Mozambican students to Harare to learn English at Ranche House College and to complete their education at one of the ZIMFEP schools.

At this time, Maryknoll Sister Jean Pruitt arrived from Dar es Salaam, Tanzania, to assist in the office. Jean was an artist and ran a project for street children in Dar. She was also a first-class fund-raiser. With Jean's help we drew up funding proposals to aid agencies for some of our activities. When she completed her volunteer work with us, Jean returned to Dar and established TAMOFA, the Tanzania Mozambique Friendship Association, that embarked on similar projects in the north of Mozambique.

In conjunction with the Governor of Manica Province in Mozambique, we decided to engage in an agricultural project that would not only grow food for the displaced but would also serve as a model of sustainable rural development in an area that was relatively safe. The Mozambique government gave us a farm in the Province and we recruited staff from Zimbabwe to manage it and to work alongside their Mozambican counterparts. Regis, I forget his second name, became the farm manager and coordinator. He remained there for almost ten years in spite of the dangers and the hardships. This solidarity farm in Vindula soon attracted international donors, one of the first being Trócaire (the Irish word for compassion), and the aid agency of the Irish bishops' conference.

Jean and I were invited to attend an international donors

conference in Maputo where we were able to report on the activities of ZIMOFA and to meet senior officials in the government. We invited Marcellino dos Santos, Vice President of Mozambique, to come to Harare to speak about the vision of FRELIMO and its successes since independence in spite of the destabilization by South Africa, the Rhodesians and RENAMO. His opening remarks to an eager audience in Harare set the stage for an informative presentation that offset the negative publicity in mainly Western media about Mozambique's socialist experiment. 'One day we will debate who had the better colonisers,' he began, to the amusement of those gathered in the large conference room. 'It won't be Mozambique,' he said to laughter as he praised the infrastructure of Harare and recounted the failure of the Portuguese to make any lasting positive contribution to the development of Mozambique.

ZIMOFA far exceeded our expectations and Fay and I gradually withdrew and let younger people take up the reigns. I was asked to return to our Maryknoll headquarters outside of New York City to head our communications office and reluctantly left Harare in 1992. My involvement with Mozambique did not end, however, as the Government of Mozambique asked me to testify before the US Congress on the situation in the country and to seek support for a peace initiative that had been initiated by the San Egidio community in Rome. This was a small but active Christian group that organized an annual Day of Prayer for Peace that brought together religious leaders of all faiths to Assisi, the birthplace of St Francis. Francis, who was hailed not only for his reverence for all creation but also for his peace initiative during the Crusades in the thirteenth century. The group also looked after the homeless and supported migrants and refugees. San Egidio acted as a catalyst in exploring ways to peace. They had the ear of the Pope and were very effective. They were instrumental in an invitation to representatives of FRELIMO and RENAMO to come to Rome several times and that led to a peace agreement in October 1992.

I testified before the US House Committee on Africa on 7 October 1992, just a few days before the signing of the Peace Accord between FRELIMO and RENAMO. In my testimony I focused on the need for assistance to repatriate refugees and displaced people, to demobilize ex-combatants on both sides, to provide psychological support to former child soldiers, to fund preparations for national elections to take place the following year, and to provide debt relief to a country that had been battered by years of conflict. I used my personal experience in Zimbabwe and Mozambique to offer examples of how this could be done.

Citing the huge toll that the conflict had taken on the civilian population, I said: 'Mozambique has become a nation in mourning. The statistics of war casualties are so enormous as to be almost inconceivable - and yet they are human beings with a face, a name, a home, family and friends who mourn their death or dislocation. In the last 16 years, more than one million people have died in war-related deaths, more than four million people have been displaced within the country and almost two million have fled to neighboring countries. What other country has lost so many people in war in recent times, young people who could have contributed to the nation's development?'

The United States government responded generously, becoming one of the major donors to the peace process in Mozambique, a country that it had shunned for years due to its socialist ideology. The peace process, however, met many obstacles and thirty years later FRELIMO and RENAMO continue to spar to the detriment of national unity and development.

President Joaquim Chissano of Mozambique, appreciative of the people-to-people links that ZIMOFA had ignited, invited me to meet him when he came to the opening session of the United Nations in 1994. Much to my surprise, my photo with him and our conversation appeared on the front page of *Noticias*, the daily newspaper in Maputo. We met again that evening at private birthday celebration for him that was organized by Roberta Washington, the architect and volunteer with whom I had stayed in Maputo in 1978. Robert van Lierop, who had organized that historic visit to Mozambique, was also present as was Francisco Madeira, the former Ambassador to Zimbabwe who had worked closely with ZIMOFA and now served as a special assistant to the President. Carlos dos Santos, another friend who had worked in the Mozambique Embassy in Zimbabwe and now worked in the President's office, was also there. The network of connections was astonishing and showed once again how effective a committed group of people can be, regardless of its size.

Thirty years later ZIMOFA continues to operate under the leadership of Dave Popatlal, who keeps alive the links between Mozambique, his birth place, and Zimbabwe, his adopted home. After Cyclone *Idai* destroyed much of the city of Beira and surrounding areas in 2019, he delivered food aid to people in need, demonstrating that home grown solutions to problems put a human face on aid and are often more effective than those of large international organizations.

18

Going Home to a Free Zimbabwe

With the closing of the School of Administration and Ideology, referred to above, my work in Mozambique seemed to come to an end. But as the last chapter shows, my involvement with Mozambique was far from over. I was expected to return to the Maryknoll Sisters' Center in Ossining, New York, and wait for a new assignment. I already knew that I wanted to go back to the new Zimbabwe to help make the change from a colonial to a liberated society. Melinda Roper, the new President of our congregation, had known me in the novitiate where she worked in the laundry and played basketball with us in her free time. She had been missioned to Central America where she witnessed the oppression of people and their desire to be free. I felt confident that when I presented the needs in Zimbabwe, she would agree that I could go there. Like her predecessor Barbara Hendricks, Melinda did not put much stress on rules and regulations but focused on our option for the poor. Like Barbara as well, she did not question where I would live or what I would do. Her main interest was in the needs of the people and the commitment of the new government to redress the wrongs of the past. We did not discuss the possibility of other sisters coming to join me at this early stage but this was my long-term plan.

I happened to be back in the States when Zimbabwe was admitted to the United Nations in September 1980. I was invited to attend the ceremony at which it became the 50th and newest member of this international body. The evening before the ceremony, I joined the Zimbabwe delegation for supper at the hotel where they were staying. I went into the kitchen and helped to prepare chicken and sadza with some of the young comrades whom I had known in Mozambique. Robert Mugabe joined the party after giving a speech in Harlem. He seemed relaxed and at ease. He asked to talk with me while the supper was being prepared. Although he was tired after a busy day, he listened to what I said about my experience in Mozambique and asked insightful questions. He suggested that I restart the School of Administration and Ideology within Zimbabwe. He welcomed me back with such warmth and enthusiasm that I was overwhelmed. It reminded me of my meeting with Tongogara in the airport and the complete trust and acceptance that I felt on both occasions. I knew I did not deserve so much credit for what I had done. I was only one of a team who happened to have been singled out for detention.

Prime Minister Mugabe then led me into the dining room to join him and senior members of the ZANU delegation for supper. After supper, he asked those present for feedback on the speech that he was to give the following day at the UN. They spoke freely and made suggestions for changes. Then he and his secretary worked on another draft of the speech. I was told that this was the fourth draft in the last few days. I was deeply impressed that he sought the advice of others and humbly and gratefully accepted their comments. I wrote to a friend in Tanzania that it was a real lesson in democracy.

Salim Salim, Tanzania's Ambassador to the UN, chaired the session at which Zimbabwe was admitted. In a moving speech, Salim mentioned how much this event meant to him personally and to Tanzania as a whole. Tanzania's President, Julius Nyerere, had played a key role in ending minority rule in Rhodesia and could be proud of this achievement. It was a real success story! I felt like dancing when I saw the beautiful gold, green and red Zimbabwean flag being raised outside the UN building. This was no easy victory. Many people had lost their lives to attain freedom and others had been tortured, imprisoned, and lost limbs. I would never take for granted this hard-won independence.

A lighter moment happened the following day when I took some members of the delegation shopping at Macy's. I was eager and excited to show them a bit of New York. I thought I had a good sense of direction and that I could find my way around on the subway. We found a station near the hotel and caught a train going in the right direction. But it was the wrong line! We all got off and started searching for the right train. By now some of the delegation were regretting they asked me to show them around. After what seemed like miles of walking through tunnels and up and down stairs, we finally got to Macy's. Finding our way around Macy's, which takes up an entire city block, was another feat. We kept getting lost on different floors and in different departments. After buying a few gifts for their wives and children, the delegation let me know that they had enough of the subway and would take a taxi back to the hotel. This shopping trip became a hilarious story that was retold and embellished on many occasions when we met later in Harare.

19

Building the New Zimbabwe

I planned to spend Christmas in Tanzania and travel from there to Harare at the beginning of the New Year, 1981. I continued to give talks to various groups about the liberation struggle in Zimbabwe and was scheduled to speak to students at Union Theological Seminary in New York City on 4 December. On the day before, word had come from El Salvador that two of our sisters were missing. On the morning of 4 December, we were called to the chapel where Sr Melinda Roper told us that the bodies of Ita Ford, Maura Clarke, Dorothy Kazel and Jean Donovan had been found buried in a shallow grave in a deserted area near the airport.

Although Maryknoll had had its share of martyrs over the years, we were not expecting it to happen in 1980. I was stunned to hear that Ita, my friend and companion who had come to Maryknoll the same year as me and went through the first three years of training with our group, had died in this brutal way. Sr Connie Pospisil and I were asked to write the letter of appreciation about her life that went out to family members and friends of Maryknoll.

I shut down my emotions and went into my head to compose

the letter. We used the words from a tape that Ita had sent her mother after her friend Carla's death in a flash flood just three months earlier.

I had images of Ita playing her guitar and singing at parties with our mutual friends, most of whom had once been in Maryknoll. She usually had a cigarette in one hand and a glass of wine in the other and was one of the first on the dance floor at parties. Ita and I had been invited to act as advisors at the Maryknoll General Assembly that took place in 1978. We had joined Sr Annette Mulry, who headed our Office of Social Concerns, to work with the group that was dealing with justice and peace. I recall Ita's prophetic words as she critiqued the first draft of their statement: 'You think it's daring to invite lay people into our (Sisters of Maryknoll) sitting rooms', she said with a touch of sarcasm. 'Within a few years some of us will die for what we believe'. These words came back to me as I reflected on what had happened. It was Ita who I had turned to when I wanted advice on whether I should go to Mozambique to work with refugees after my imprisonment and deportation from Rhodesia. In her laid back and somewhat sardonic way, Ita challenged me, 'Why would you even consider saying no?'

While I was pondering Ita's influence on my life, I debated whether I should cancel the engagement at Union Theological. I doubted if I could concentrate on anything and might break down in tears. I had little time to decide since I had to get the train into the city and then a subway north to 125th St. Instead of speaking about Zimbabwe, I told the students about the death of the four women and of the struggle for liberation in El Salvador that was not unlike that in Zimbabwe. I don't know if I made any sense. I collapsed exhausted on the train to return to Ossining from the city that evening.

A few days later, I was given the privilege of reading a passage from scripture at the memorial service that was held at the

Maryknoll seminary chapel in memory of Ita and Maura. I had the privilege again the following Sunday, when I read one of the lessons at the Mass held at St Patrick's Cathedral in memory of the four women. My parents had come to the city on a tour and were present at this Mass. We said our good-byes on the steps of the cathedral, not knowing when we would see each other again. Perhaps the death of our sisters and friends made this farewell even more difficult than usual. I hugged each of my parents and tried to smile so they wouldn't worry about me.

The morning of my departure for the African continent, Archbishop Dom Helder Camara of Recife, Brazil, said the Mass in our chapel where he spoke of the risk of martyrdom when we stand with the poor. I was sent on my way with the blessings of prophets and martyrs and the uncertainly of what would happen when I returned to the country from which I had been deported three years earlier. I wrote the following reflection on the meaning of Ita's life and death as I left the safety of our Center in the States to return to the newly independent Zimbabwe:

In the last letter I wrote to Ita Ford, I said, 'You give me strength and courage'. When Ita was home on her reflection year, we used to share our experiences of Chile and Rhodesia. There was no need to explain what it means for your neighbors and friends to disappear, be tortured or killed. Ita had lived through it in Chile.

Without preaching or being pious, but by the example of her life, she called me to live more simply, more completely with the poor. I take her with me to Zimbabwe, and I pray to her for my companions and myself:

> *Ita, help us to love the poor as you did.*
> *Give us the strength to overcome our fears;*
> *to get up and keep going after disappointments and*
> *tragedies.*
> *Give us the strength to keep trying to build a world of*

justice and sharing.
Give us the courage to oppose unjust structures in this
world which have caused your death; the courage to
do and speak the truth.
And let our love, like yours, be not just words and
talk, but true love which shows itself in action.

My arrival in Salisbury, soon to be renamed Harare, was
another adventure. I had written ahead to Fidelis Mukonori SJ, to
let him know I was coming and to arrange a place for me to stay.
I could see no sign of him when I exited the airport and instead
found Fay Chung, whom I knew from the camps in Mozambique,
waiting for me. She took me to her uncle's house in an affluent
part of the city and he welcomed me to stay in a guest cottage on
the grounds of his property. Fay and her extended family would
become my family too. At that time, Fay was still attached to the
Education department of the Party, ZANU-PF, but she would soon
be appointed the head of planning in the Ministry of Education
and would preside over the expansion of the education system to
the most neglected parts of the country.

Dzingai Mutumbuka had become the first black Minister of
Education in the new Zimbabwe. He and Fay prepared a job
description for me that included helping to set up an educational
organization that would build schools for former refugees and
war veterans. I was also asked to work with the new honorary
President of independent Zimbabwe, Canaan Banana, to establish
a school for war veterans of both liberation armies, ZANLA, led
by Mugabe, and ZIPRA under Joshua Nkoma. President Banana
was a Methodist minister who had spent time in prison during the
liberation war and had helped mobilize support for the liberation
struggle within the country. He was also an Ndebele from the
west of the country. At Independence, he was seen as someone
non-threatening who could help to unite the country and prevent

violence between the various liberation armies and factions.

I was given an office at State House, an imposing colonial building surrounded by beautiful gardens in the heart of Harare. Each day the entire staff had tea together on the verandah of this charming structure that also housed the President, his wife Janet, and their children. Martin, the youngest rode his tricycle up and down the corridors of this stately residence, bringing laughter to a serious and hard-working staff.

At one of the morning tea breaks, a young white man who was a security officer for the President approached me. 'Do you remember me', he asked, with a sheepish smile. I racked my brain trying to think. Seeing my confusion, he said, 'I'm Officer Bacon'. Then I remembered. He was one of the special branch officers who arrested me and took me to prison. I smiled in recognition and took his extended hand to shake it. Looking me in the eyes, he stated: 'You were right. We believed our own propaganda'. I was astounded at this confession and his humility to admit his mistake. This was not the only time I met some of my former captors and received their heartfelt apology, as if asking for my understanding and forgiveness. I believed that this was a good omen for reconciliation in the country as a whole. The new government retained many of the white officials who had worked for the former regime. When I questioned this, I was told that they had experience and were prepared to accept change.

The President himself was shy and quiet. When I presented him with ideas for curriculum and staffing, he asked relevant questions and made helpful suggestions, but rarely joked or engaged in small talk. We worked well together and soon had everything needed to begin. Banana had purchased a farm to the east of Marondera for the school. Pre-fab classrooms and dormitories were put up on the grounds and staff were recruited from both ZANLA and ZIPRA. The school, to be called Kushinga-Phikelela, meaning 'perseverance' in Shona and Ndebele, was to be an agricultural college and a secretarial school. My experience with the ZANU School of Administration and Ideology was to guide the secretarial school.

With the infrastructure in place, I was sent with two senior commanders from ZANLA and ZIPRA to an Assembly Point1 in Midlands to recruit the female students for the secretarial college. I accepted the cultural norms at the time that expected women to work in offices rather than on farms. Even though women in the rural areas were excellent farmers, at that time they were not included in the agricultural program.

We stopped at the Air Force base in Gweru for a break and something to eat on our way to the assembly point. I marveled as I listened to the joking between the white soldiers who had been in the Rhodesian army and my companions, Comrades Jele and Bangidza, who had fought against them. As they exchanged stories of battles and close calls with death, asking each other how they escaped, I sat mute in wonder. After we left, I queried, 'How could you laugh and joke with the former enemy about life and death issues?' 'It was war', they replied. 'We were only doing our duty and they were doing theirs.' I hoped that this spirit of camaraderie would survive as the reality of the changes required in society would begin to sink in.

The women that we interviewed at the Assembly Point spoke English and had completed at least two years of secondary school before they joined the struggle. Some had risen to senior positions in the respective liberation armies and were very confident and outspoken. We recruited an equal number from the two liberation forces and were satisfied that the first intake of secretarial students would be stars.

---

1   Assembly points were locations scattered round the country where guerrillas gathered after the ceasefire was signed in December 1979. It took time to disband them as many administrative details had to be worked out.

President Banana choose the heads of the two schools: Felix Mavhondo and Abraham Madiwa became the Principle and Deputy of the entire complex while Misheck Ngwenya, who had been the Production Manager at Mambo Press, the Catholic publishing house in Gweru, became the head of the commercial school. Two others became heads of the agricultural college and Mr Rambire, who had worked for the former white commercial farmer, became the farm manager. It was agreed that all students and staff would spend one day a week in the fields since the secretarial students were expected to work in rural district offices where knowledge of farming would be helpful. We also agreed to include students in the running of the school and to have frequent meetings where ideas and complaints could be heard.

I was surprised that the students wanted to have prayer meetings and Bible discussion groups. Mr Mwadiwa, who was an active layman in the Methodist church, usually led these weekly meetings. He also arranged for us to attend services at churches in and around Marondera where the former freedom fighters would tell their stories, helping to allay the fears of the local community. Memories of the war were still fresh and not everyone was comfortable having more than one hundred 'terrorists' in the neighborhood. These church visits opened the door to cordial relations and helping hands from the area.

Regular staff meetings were held to share information about the day-to-day running of the school and to instill revolutionary principles. When news reached us of fighting between troops from the two liberation movements at a military base outside of Bulawayo in early 1982, we feared that the same thing could happen between our students. President Banana visited the school and delivered a message of unity. The students from the respective military wings of ZANU and ZAPU continued to socialize and work together. There was never even a hint of division between them.

I credit Canaan Banana as well as the staff for preventing violence from spreading to this experimental project and destroying one of its main reasons for existing.

Although there were no conflicts between ZANLA and ZIPRA, we sometimes experienced conflicts between the male and female students. The women were not only smart but also very attractive and the men were naturally attracted to them. Perhaps forgetting that the woman had received military training, the male students sometimes had to run for their lives if they dared to propose love to a women or comment on her looks. One particular incident stands out since we had to provide sanctuary in our staff house for one of the girls who landed a few well-placed kicks to the groin of a romantic pursuer. After this humiliation, he vowed to get revenge so we invited the student to stay with us until emotions cooled off.

I shared a staff house with two other staff members, Dianne Yates, a teacher from New Zealand, and Cookie Chinamano, a young woman whose parents were leaders within ZAPU and had a long history of opposing colonialism. I had earlier shared a smaller dwelling at the institute with Memory Mabaya, an instructor from ZANLA, and her baby daughter Chipo. These teachers entered fully into the ethos of the new school and contributed to the development of relevant curriculum that fit the new situation in the country. In fact, Dianne's typing exercises were published as a commercial textbook by Mambo Press since the examples that she used made so much more sense than the former books that used examples from Britain.

My favorite day of the week at Kushinga was the one we spent in the fields working alongside the agricultural students. Before going to the fields, we were given a briefing on the work for the day; picking tobacco or slaughtering and dressing chickens, or harvesting maize and groundnuts. Lunch was brought to us in the fields so that we could spend as much of the day as possible doing the required work. Coming from an urban background, I appreciated experiencing rural life and learning how to farm, even if it was for a short time. I was able to cut off a chicken's head without fainting and to douse it in hot water to make it easy to pluck the feathers. I could shell peanuts with my fingers although I was twice as slow as everyone else and I learned which tobacco leaves were ready to pick and be cured. President Banana often joined us for these days in the field, donning overalls and a cap like everyone else. At the end of the day, we would collapse hot and dirty into the shower and then get an early supper and go to bed.

We organized open days at Kushinga when many of the government ministers joined us in the fields. It was modeled after the traditional custom of *nhimbe* when neighbors would help each other with the chores. This practice of communal labor brought to mind the Acts of the Apostles and Robert Mugabe's words to me that this sharing of life in common was the model of socialism that Zimbabwe would adopt.

20

Coming Home to a Cold Reception: Zimbabwe Project

Not all war veterans were as fortunate as those who were recruited to study at Kushinga Phikelela. Instead of receiving a hero's welcome when they returned to their homes, many of these young soldiers were shunned by neighbors and even by their own families who had suffered during the war and had become destitute after feeding the guerrillas from the little that they had. Many had been arrested, beaten and tortured by the colonial government for assisting the 'terrorists' while others had been placed in encampments, known as protected villages, to isolate them from the guerrilla forces. Others had witnessed or participated in the brutal murders of those who had been accused of being informers for the Smith government. Labelled 'sell-outs', they were tortured and murdered at the all-night rallies or *pungwes* to send a warning to others that this was the fate of traitors. Because of these experiences, many people feared the war veterans and were reluctant to welcome them back into the communities that they had left many years before. They also were surprised to find that their sons and daughters returned empty-handed, without bringing any remuneration for all that had been lost.

War veterans with secondary education were recruited into the new national army but those who left school when very young to join the struggle were left to fend for themselves. The government had set up a war veterans fund and an office to assist them that was manned by officials from both ZANU and ZAPU but the funds were very limited and there were allegations of corruption at the office.

Concerned about the fate of these young people who had sacrificed everything to fight for freedom for their country, some non-governmental organisations and churches turned their attention to assist them. The Zimbabwe Project, with whom I had worked in Mozambique, asked me to do a survey among the newly appointed government leaders, many of whom I had known in Mozambique, whether they thought we should continue our mission or should shut down. Without exception, every government minister that I interviewed, urged the Zimbabwe Project to continue and suggested that it focus on these neglected war veterans. Judith Todd, who had already done some work with the ZP in Zambia and had been imprisoned by the Smith regime for her support of the liberation movements, became the project director. She was passionate about assisting these abandoned youth, was brilliant at fund-raising and also a pro at gaining good publicity. Two war veterans from each of the main political parties joined her on the staff: Morris Mtsambiwa, who had been one of the teachers at the ZANLA School in Maputo, and Aiden Thwala, a ZAPU comrade who had been in the Education Department in Zambia. A fourth member of staff was John Conradie who was, as we have seen, detained for twelve years by the Smith government for assisting the 'terrorists'. I was a member of the board together with several others including representatives of agencies that were also giving support to war veterans.

The focus of the ZP was adult education and cooperatives. John Conradie helped to set up a course in adult literacy in Mbare with the assistance of Kathy Stewart and Ntombi Nyathi. This course prepared teams of war veterans that would run literacy courses in urban townships and rural villages. The ZP avoided the cooking and sewing classes that had been offered at the ZANU Women's Center in Maputo and trained women for leadership roles in rural communities similar to those courses in administration being offered at Kushinga-Phikelela.

Rural development was a focus of the new government and it embarked on a modest land reform program under the Ministry of Lands and Resettlement that was headed by Sam Geza, a war veteran who had been detained in Mozambique for his leftist leanings but had remained with ZANU on his release. Groups of war veterans were eligible to apply for land that they would farm together cooperatively. The ZP provided some training and support for these fledgling operations and was instrumental in setting up the Organisation of Collective Cooperatives in Zimbabwe (OCCZIM). This organization was launched at Cold Comfort Farm, a well-known cooperative farm that had survived the war under the leadership of Cephas Muropa and Guy and Molly Clutton-Brock. I took the minutes at this launch and attended many subsequent meetings that were often chaired by Cde Mtsambiwa.

Two of the outstanding cooperatives that came under the tutelage of the Zimbabwe Project were *Vukuzenzele* and *Shandisai Pfungwa*. *Vukuzenzele* was set up for injured ZIPRA ex-combatants on land donated by Senator Garfield Todd, Judith's father, on his ranch in Shurugwi. Judith visited the farm regularly and helped the young men and women make a go of this unique project for the physically handicapped. *Shandisai Pfungwa* was situated on a former commercial farm outside of Marondera in Mashonaland East. John Conradie put his efforts into this project and helped the group set up agroindustry projects in bakery and leather work.

I was called upon to take the minutes at the annual general meeting of this cooperative and to be the scrutineer at the election of its leadership. I remember being put off by the general state of the farm house where the members were living. The windows were broken, toilets no longer flushed, no furniture but only mats on the floor for sleeping. It took me time to accept that young men and women who had been sleeping on the ground under the trees during the war would find this rundown farmhouse quite luxurious! I found the members very delightful and often visited the farm on my way to and from Kushinga Phikelela.

In spite of all the training and the funds put into this project, the farming side was never very successful. None of the members had grown tobacco before nor had they grown up with more than an acre of land. A commercial enterprise of several hundred acres was not familiar territory. The farm workers remained on the farm but we soon learned that they were used to getting orders from the former white 'boss' and would make no decisions on their own. Very soon the relationship between the more educated and much younger war veterans and the older less educated laborers deteriorated to the point that no work was being done.

There were also power struggles between the members for leadership of the cooperative. Little by little, members drifted away and it looked as if this experiment in cooperative living and farming was a non starter. This was a huge disappointment to John Conradie who had invested so much time, energy and love into this project and its members.

Not easily discouraged, however, John created the Kushanda Project, an initiative that provided early education for pre-school children in the rural areas around Marondera. The project included a community library that would serve as a prototype for other such libraries around the country. With a generous grant from the Van Leer Foundation, Kushanda Project took off and became a model for early childhood education and was the recipient of an international award. Not long after this achievement, John discovered that he had a brain tumor and he began to make plans for his final days. He chose to stay in Marondera where he was looked after by some of the war veterans who had been with him in prison. I had become close to John and we would sometimes meet in a small hotel in Greendale on the outskirts of Harare for a gin and tonic and a chat about what was happening in the country. Disillusioned by the rampant corruption and the departure from a socialist orientation, John often gave the example of the black widow spider that devoured its mate, comparing it to the revolution that ended up destroying what it had once embraced. One of the last times that I visited him, he told me that he didn't want to be a burden to anyone and to accept his suffering and death quietly. His wish was granted as he passed away peacefully at his home with only his faithful caregivers in attendance. The government named him a national provincial war hero and he was buried with honors in the local cemetery in Marondera.

Judith Todd kept the Zimbabwe Project alive after John and others had left and some of the projects such as Shandisai Pfungwa had collapsed. *Vukuzenzele* and some of the other projects were more successful and the ZP continued to have an impact. When the government accepted the demands of war veterans for a monthly pay check, the Zimbabwe Project shifted its focus to promote development projects in impoverished rural communities, putting into practice the lessons that it had learned in responding to the needs of the war veterans immediately after the end of the war. I had great admiration and respect for the war veterans that I knew and had worked with and was proud to have played a small part in this initiative to assist them to contribute in a meaningful way to the creation of a new Zimbabwe.

21

New Schools for a New Zimbabwe: ZIMFEP

When I interviewed ZANU's Secretary for Education, Dzingai Mutumbuka, in Mozambique, he spoke of his dream of transforming education in Zimbabwe by moving away from the exam-oriented British system and embracing a system that would be better suited to the country's rural economy. As the first Minister of Education in independent Zimbabwe, he discovered that bringing change to an entrenched system would not be so easy. Not only did the civil servants in the Ministry have a vested interest in maintaining the colonial education system but the parents likewise wanted their children to get a first-class, education, meaning British. They all lobbied for the Cambridge exam system to be maintained. Rather than fight against this significant group, Minister Mutumbuka chose to go around it by creating an independent organization that would pioneer educational experiments. The Zimbabwe Foundation for Education with Production (ZIMFEP) was established with his

1111111

blessing and full support but it had no staff and no funds – only a mandate to experiment.

It was my job to help make it happen. I had the Minister's full support and a wonderful board of people who had been part of the educational experiments in Mozambique and Zambia. They included Fay Chung, who had headed the teacher training program in Mozambique and was now the head of planning in the Ministry of Education; Roma Nyathi, an official with ZAPU who had been involved in the schools in Zambia; Sam Geza who had been arrested and imprisoned by ZANU for his radical views but who was now in charge of the resettlement program in the Ministry of Lands and Resettlement; Taka Mudariki, who was an adult educator and now worked in the Ministry of Education. They all knew far more than I did but they already had full time jobs in government.

I was fully behind the concept of marrying academic and practical subjects. St Lawrence O'Toole School in Pittsburgh prepared us for the world of work and introduced us to various professions. We visited local factories such as Heinz and learned about the different products that Heinz made and were given samples to taste of the tomato juice and the pickles. It was a favorite annual outing. In our last two years in primary school, we attended practical lessons at a nearby public school. The girls did sewing and cooking while the boys did carpentry and drafting. I learned how to make my own clothes and to cook a decent meal, including setting the table and making decorations for special occasions. Although I would never be a competent homemaker, I enjoyed these classes, especially getting to eat the food that we prepared.

In high school, those of us in the science stream attended special classes at Westinghouse Corporation on Saturdays where leading scientists introduced us to concepts such as nuclear energy that would become a focus of Westinghouse in the future. While some of these lessons were way over my head, they gave me an appreciation of the scope of local industries. The best of the students were hired by Westinghouse to pioneer these products.

Career counseling was also part of the curriculum. Local professionals spoke to our high school class each month, introducing us to their profession and letting us know what was required. I could not imagine a school that was not linked to future careers. The British system of rote learning, exams and a class system that favored academic over practical education made little sense to me. I was, therefore, happy to be part of an experiment to do away with it and to link learning with work.

From the start, ZIMFEP included students and teachers from both ZANU and ZAPU. I began by visiting the various centers where the former refugees were being accommodated until the new schools were built. I travelled the length and breadth of the country and saw that we had to move fast if we were not to have riots on our hands and teachers and students absconding. Although the government was providing food, the students were overcrowded in churches, school dormitories and even in tents. They were worse off than they had been in the camps outside the country and complaints were growing louder.

One of the holding centers was Fatima School in Lupane that was under the auspices of the Catholic Church. Fr Nigel Johnson, SJ, who had stayed with the refugees in Zambia, accompanied me to meet Bishop Karlen, the head of the church in Matabeleland. The diocese had suffered much damage during the war and Bishop Schmidt, his predecessor had been shot and killed on the road by guerrillas of ZIPRA who tended to be more hostile to religion than were their counterparts in ZANLA. The negative experience during the war made the bishop wary of collaborating with people whom he saw as Marxists who would suppress religion. Nigel and

I eventually convinced him that these were children of Zimbabwe who needed education and a place to stay. Bishop Karlen agreed that ZIMFEP could have the school as long as we left the church and the neighboring parish intact. The Ministry of Education paid something to the diocese and we never had any further problems with the church.

The ZIMFEP board bought a small house in the Avenues of Harare that served as our office. The staff consisted of George Mandipaza from ZANU who I had known at Matenje camp in Mozambique and Aiden Thwala, from ZAPU who was recommended by Matthew Mtobi, one of the teachers from the schools in the camps in Zambia who would become the headmaster of a future ZIMFEP school. We recruited the office secretary from the first class of graduates from Kushinga Phikelela. Revd Ed Morrow and his wife Lorraine joined us after they were deported from Namibia. Ed was not only a pastor but a builder and took on the task of supervising the construction of eight schools while Lorraine assisted with the secretarial work in the office.

Initially, I commuted from Kushinga in Marondera to spend three days in the ZIMFEP office and three at Kushinga. My task was to meet with donors and to raise funds while Fay Chung, Taka Mudariki along with Victoria Chitepo, deputy Minister of Education, secured the land on which to build the schools. We started with Chindinduma in Shamva where a Danish group of volunteers, 'People to People', were on site to assist in the construction and with Rusununguko in Bromley that had been acquired by Patrick van Rensburg who had set up the Foundation for Education with Production in Botswana and had built two schools there. Van Rensburg was a pioneer in the field and while we valued his expertise and experience, we discovered that we differed over the running of the schools and their ownership. The board reached an amicable settlement with Patrick and he agreed to focus on Botswana and to let ZIMFEP run the schools in Zimbabwe.

The differences with People to People were more difficult to resolve. This group had assisted ZANU during the struggle and were well meaning but the young Danish volunteers had little or no training in construction and little knowledge of the local culture. As a result, they clashed with the headmaster and teachers of both the primary and secondary schools. We met with the leaders of the organization and politely asked them to remove their volunteers from Chindinduma. They reluctantly agreed.

Each of the eight schools had its unique history and identity. We had three in Matabeleland under ZAPU heads and teachers: J.Z. Moyo in West Nicholson, George Silundika in Nyamandlovu and Fatima in Lupane. The schools under ZANU were Chindinduma, Rusun.unguko, Nkululelo in Midlands and Mavhudzi in Nyazura. I compiled a book about ZIMFEP that goes into more detail about each project.[1]

I mention only two incidents that stand out for me. I had been an ardent supporter of community-based theater in Kenya that had been pioneered by the writer Ngugi wa Thiongo and two associates, Ngugi wa Mirii and Kimani Gecau. The Kenyan government felt threatened by the movement and burnt down the outdoor theater in Limuru, an influential Kikuyu suburb outside of Nairobi, and arrested wa Thiongo. I was asked to help wa Mirii and Gecau escape and arranged for our sisters in Nairobi to buy air tickets for them to come to Harare. Minister Mutumbuka liked the idea of introducing community-based theater in ZIMFEP schools and agreed to assign the two Kenyans to Chindinduma School in Shamva.

Wa Mirii and Gecau fitted into the rural setting and reached out to the neighboring community in adjoining farms as well

1 McLaughlin, Janice with V Nhundu, P Mlambo and F Chung, *Schools That Work: The History of ZIMFEP*, ZIMFEP, Harare, 1994.

as to the students at Chindinduma Secondary School. Together they rehearsed an original play about the military leader of the liberation struggle against the British in Kenya. Called *The Trial of Dedan Kimathi*, the story bore some resemblance to the liberation struggle in Zimbabwe and the play was extremely popular in Shamva and wherever it was performed.

Another play that was written by the students was more controversial. It highlighted the grievances that students had against the headmaster who was also a war veteran. He was portrayed as a dictator who was abusing school property as well as students. The students and their mentors should have expected the headmaster's reaction to this negative image. Outraged, he closed the project and expelled the two Kenyans from the school. This was by no means the end of community-based theatre as wa Mirii went on to open a nation-wide program that was supported by the Ministry of Youth and Culture while Gecau joined the English Department at the University of Zimbabwe. I was chastened by this disaster and no longer felt welcome at Chindinduma until the headmaster was transferred to another school.

More chilling were events at the three schools in Matabeleland during the terrible period of Gukurahundi, when the Fifth Brigade terrorized the people in the area in their campaign against those they called dissidents. I received a phone call that Matthew Mtobi, the headmaster of the school in Nyamandlovu, had been arrested. I called some of the army commanders that I had known in Mozambique and was told that Mtobi was accused of feeding dissidents at the school, a very serious offense that could bring lifetime imprisonment or even death. I made a decision to travel to Bulawayo to try to see him in prison and to talk to those in charge in the military. I was not allowed into the prison so I went to the office of the army commander at the time, Constantine Chiwenga. He welcomed me and listened to my defense of Mtobi. A few days later Mtobi was released from prison. He told me that he knew that the dissidents were hiding in the forest near the school and came out at night to steal food. If he had intervened, he thought they might abduct students and also destroy the school. The school continued to operate but was probably under surveillance. Mtobi stayed on as head and was a calming influence in the midst of chaos and violence.

Not long after this, two teachers from the school who had been attending a ZIMFEP workshop in Harare for new teachers disappeared. We put them on the bus to Bulawayo but they never arrived at the school. I phoned contacts in the army again and was told that they probably had gone to Botswana. I assumed that they had been abducted and murdered but I had no proof. It was my word or my assumption against the word of senior military personnel.

Tragedy struck again at the school with the brutal and gruesome murder of Martin Olds, a neighboring farmer who provided the school with water and with meat while his wife helped to set up the library. The Olds were a family that had accepted the changes brought about by independence and opted to help their neighbors. Headmaster Mtobi and Martin Olds struck up a friendship and Mtobi often called on Mr Olds for help. A group of armed men surrounded Mr Olds at his farmhouse. He had sent his wife, who was in a wheelchair, to stay in Bulawayo, where it was safer. Olds defended himself and was shot and killed at the entrance to his home. I wrote an impassioned letter to the press, decrying this senseless murder, one of thousands at the time. I was powerless and a letter to the press was meaningless yet it made me feel better. Should I have gone to the bishops, to the international media, to the leaders of the government about these and other incidents? Was I complicit in these crimes for not raising the alarm and alerting those who might do something about it? I will go to my grave with these sins of omission weighing on my conscience.

The sequel to events at George Silundika School offered some hope that the violence would not be repeated. After the Unity Accord was signed between ZANU and ZAPU in 1987, I travelled with Senator Joseph Culverwell, Deputy Minister of Education, to the school in Nyamandlovu for a ceremony to acknowledge what had happened and to allow the school to continue without any further disturbance. Flint Magama, military commander in the area, mesmerized us with his honesty and humility. Speaking in Ndebele, Shona and English he admitted the mistakes that had been made and asked for pardon. We were surprised and reassured by his words and also by his openness and willingness to confess in public. Years later, he had a senior role in defeating RENAMO in Mozambique and died there in a helicopter crash. I mourned this loss for the country and for the region.

The concept of education with production made sense but was never fully implemented. In addition to opposition from many quarters, ZIMFEP itself was a weak institution without sufficient resources or staff to make a significant difference. The Board had brilliant ideas but had little knowledge of the reality on the ground. Teachers from the struggle were not accepted by the government and were often transferred with little notice; some suffered from post-traumatic stress and relied on traditional ceremonies for healing; teachers posted by the government had little interest in our experiments and only focused on exam results; each school depended on the one in charge for direction and guidance – some did better than others; international teachers from Germany and Denmark were hard-working and well-meaning but had little influence and were only there for a few years. The ZIMFEF staff worked tirelessly and were often disappointed by the results.

Our major success was the construction of the schools under the leadership of Rev. Ed Morrow. Ed hired local builders who knew what they were doing, were honest and capable. Ed travelled to the schools to monitor progress while I raised the money and kept the donors informed. Each school was unique in design and implementation. Much depended on the creativity and the interest of the headmasters and their deputies as well as the farm managers that ZIMFEP employed.

ZIMFEP added Mupfure College, a skills training center in Chegutu. Matthew Mtobi had joined me in the Education Department of ZIMFEP. We made it our goal to train the teachers and other staff at Mupfure, learning from the mistakes we had made at the other schools. The fact that Mupfure came directly under ZIMFEP made it easier to experiment. The teachers and staff were open to change and this became our star project.

In the years that I was the coordinator of ZIMFEP, I focused on raising funds, building the schools and training teachers in the concept of Education with Production. I also drafted speeches for senior officials that gave examples of what it meant and that helped to spread the concept in the media. When Taka Mudariki replaced me as coordinator I stayed on to focus on teacher training and publications. We initiated a newspaper, *Teach and Learn*, and published about a dozen books, the last being the history of ZIMFEP.

Looking back, I realize that my tendency to go directly to the Minister of Education, bypassing officials in the Ministry of Education, did not make me popular within the Ministry. Trying to juggle eight schools in different parts of the country was a feat. The farms were even more problematic. ZIMFEP employed a coordinator for the farms who would visit and give advice to the farm managers. They were given large tracts of land and a work force of students but produced very little. Aside from the cattle ranch at J.Z. Moyo School in West Nicholson that was managed by Karl Goeppert, a German who had been hired by the Lutheran

World Federation, our other farms had limited results.

When Dzingai Mutumbuka left the Ministry over the Willowgate scandal, nothing was ever the same. He had been a vocal and effective advocate of education with production. Although the ZIMFEP board members were committed, they did not have the same weight as Mutumbuka and had their own work to do. I left ZIMFEP toward the end of the 1980s when the country embraced structural adjustment, opening the door to corruption and bringing to an end the leadership code and other attempts to instill a sense of honesty and personal sacrifice in government. The values of the liberation struggle were being swept under the carpet and replaced by the capitalist values that were also undermining equality and justice in my home country. I look back with nostalgia on the vision of those early days of independence and on the hard work and sacrifice of so many young people with whom I was privileged to work. I wonder if they also shed tears at what has become of the dream.

22

With the People: Tafara Township

From childhood, I imagined living and working on the African continent and staying in a mud-walled and thatched hut without running water or electricity, much as the millions on this continent live. My concept of mission was to be one with the people whom we served; to share their joys and sorrows. I knew that with my college education and access to US dollars, I would never be able to experience the hardships and uncertainties they faced, but at least I wanted to narrow the gap between us. I had a taste of a simpler life when I lived in refugee camps in Mozambique where I slept on a bed of sticks, bathed in a small bucket of water and had little to eat. This was only for a short time, however. I yearned to experience the life of the majority of Zimbabweans rather than living in a middle-class neighborhood with most of the amenities that I would have in the United States.

The opportunity came in 1987 when Maryknoll Sister, Kathryn Shannon, who shared my dream, agreed to live with me in one of the African townships that surrounded the capital of Harare. Kathryn was teaching disabled war veterans at Danhiko School that had been established especially for them by an American volunteer, Sharon Ladin, and located not far from the Rehabilitation Center in Ruwa where many of them lived. Kathryn had begun her missionary service as a teacher in Hawaii but after many years there she asked to be transferred to Tanzania to work with people more in need. Her passion for justice and concern for the poor were legendary as were her frequent letters to the Pope and other world leaders to correct this or that issue. In Tanzania she worked with the Maasai people and lived in a trailer on the edge of the Rift Valley. Her close encounters with wild animals in this rugged terrain made for hilarious stories at Maryknoll meetings where Kathryn stole the show. When Zimbabwe was opened as a new mission after Independence, Kathryn was one of the first to volunteer, always ready to try something new and challenging.

She lived with the Dominican Sisters in Harare while I lived with my good friend Fay Chung, her daughter Chipo, as well as Fungai, the young sister of Irene Mahamba (Comrade Ropa). I loved being surrogate mother to Chipo and Fungai when Fay, as head of planning in the Ministry of Education, travelled throughout the country, establishing schools in neglected rural areas. Chipo, Fungai and I baked cookies on the weekends and went swimming at a local municipal pool. When Fay was home we visited war veterans that we knew or invited them for a meal at the flat where we lived. Vice President Simon Muzenda and Education Minister Dzingai Mutumbaka were frequent guests at these gatherings where Fay baked chicken and potatoes and I put together a salad and desert.

I became an adopted member of Fay's extended Chinese family and enjoyed the perks of delicious Chinese meals at the home of her sister on the weekends as well as invitations to Chinese feasts by the Embassy. Kathryn and I were both content in our work and our living situations but circumstances were leading us in another direction. When the Dominican Sisters moved to another house and Fay did the same, it was time to take the leap into another world .

The townships that ringed the city of Harare were a result of the colonial policy that restricted Africans from owning property in the city center and its suburbs. Cooks, gardeners and domestic staff of the white community could live in the servants' quarters that were a common feature at the back of the main house but otherwise Africans were forbidden to live in these all-white areas. This separation of the races, a form of apartheid, resulted in large settlements of low-income housing on the periphery of urban areas throughout the country.

When we decided to move to one of these townships, Kathryn called Fr Tony Path, the pastor of St Alphonsus Parish in Tafara, a township on the far east side of Harare. Kathryn's brother was a member of the Redemptorist community in the United States so it was natural for her to approach another Redemptorist. 'Sr Janice and I would like to move into a house in the township', she told him, 'Is Tafara a possibility?' Fr Path was instantly enthusiastic and said that he would get back to her. Within a few hours he called to say he had a house for us to rent and we would be most welcome. We decided to consult Bishop Patrick Mutume, Secretary General of the Zimbabwe Catholic Bishops' Conference and a friend. 'Should we ask the Archbishop if we can move to a township?' 'You know that he will say no. Move first and then inform him'. With these wise words, we moved into the township toward the end of 1987.

The house that we rented from the family of a local Redemptorist priest, was made of prefabricated cement walls and an asbestos roof. It had two bedrooms, a sitting room and small kitchen. The house was roasting hot in the summer months and freezing cold in the winter. An outdoor toilet and shower with cold water were attached to the back of the house. The best feature was a huge avocado tree in the front yard that attracted the children in the neighborhood who climbed to the top branches to pick the ripe fruit for us in exchange for a share of it for themselves.

Our house was opposite Hurudza Beer Hall, another colonial relic that was owned by the City Council and earned income for the city from the sale of beer and from music concerts that brought large crowds to dance and sing until the early hours of the morning. Some of Zimbabwe's leading musicians entertained us on weekends with their music and we often crossed the road to join in the dancing and singing with our neighbors.

We moved in on a Saturday with the help of some of the youth leaders of the parish who became our mentors and protectors. The house had no electricity so we had borrowed a two-burner gas hotplate from some friends to cook our meals. Neither Kathryn nor I had ever used a gas hotplate before but we had to learn fast as visitors were due just a few hours after we were settled. Fr Jack Corcoran, a Maryknoll priest who worked in Nepal had come to Zimbabwe to visit his sister, Anne, a member of the Religious of the Sacred Heart of Mary (RSHM). Anne, Jack and two other sisters arrived just as the sun was setting. In the glow of candlelight, we served sodas and peanuts while we struggled to cook chicken and potatoes in the dark.

An evening of laughter and burnt food with international visitors was the perfect christening of our new home. Kathryn and I fell into a deep sleep, expecting to wake up about 9 a.m. to attend the 10 a.m. Mass at the parish. A loud knock on our metal door at 7, had us both jumping out of bed to see who was there. We were met by a delegation of men and women from the local branch of the ruling Party, ZANU. They welcomed us and politely informed us that we were expected to attend the ZANU party meeting that took place once a month a few streets from where we lived. It was clear that we couldn't refuse. We threw on some clothes and followed our guides to a large gathering seated on the ground in an open clearing by the side of a house.

This was our second christening in less than 24 hours as we were introduced to the crowd and expected to say a few words. I stumbled through some greetings in Shona and said something about how happy we were to be their neighbors and asking for their help in getting acquainted with local life. I sat down feeling very inadequate and foolish and waited to hear what my companion would say. Kathryn rattled off the history of the Monomutapa Empire in perfect Shona, telling them that the success of the empire was the result of religion and politics existing in harmony. I held my breath as I wondered where this was leading when Kathryn delivered the punch line. 'This meeting is on a Sunday morning when Christians have their religious services. We will attend but will leave when it is time for us to go to the Mass at 10.'

From that day onward, at about 9:45 the chairman would announce: 'It's time for the Sisters and other Christians to attend their services.' With this introduction we became well known and were invited to every major event, be it the birth of a child, the death of a neighbor or the graduation of a student. Each year as the anniversary of Independence rolled around, I was elected as treasurer and sent to buy the refreshments for the celebration.

Our introduction to the parish was equally rewarding. Fr Path and the members of the parish council welcomed us wholeheartedly and accepted us as partners in parish ministry. Kathryn took on the training of catechists and became an advisor to the youth and women's groups. I continued to commute to the ZIMFEP office in the city during the day and on evenings and weekends I participated fully in community activities.

We assisted the youth to set up a poultry project as well as a stone-carving cooperative while we encouraged the women to start a sewing group. With our connections, we were able to send a few young people to be apprenticed with leading stone carvers in the country while we obtained orders from a textile factory for the women to make garments for export. On my next visit to the States, I was thrilled to see our Tafara products being displayed and sold at leading department stores in Manhattan. Just as amazing was seeing the work of some of our youthful stone carvers on permanent display at the airport in Atlanta, Georgia. These were success stories beyond our wildest imagination.

We were feeling more at home each day and gave thanks that we had made the move to this urban location of about 20,000 families. Tafara Township had been built in the mid-50s to provide housing for workers at the nearby cement factory and for maids, cooks and gardeners for Greendale and other white suburbs on the eastern side of Harare. The people were not destitute. Most of the men had a job and could afford to buy food, pay rent and send their children to school. It was not so different from the working-class neighborhood where I grew up although the amenities such as electricity and indoor plumbing were absent. In the first decade of independence, schools and health clinics functioned well and served the people in their vicinity. The Ministry of Social Welfare also catered for the needs of the poor and marginalized. Churches provided not only spiritual nourishment but also offered activities for youth, women and men. Some of the women ran a crèche for pre-school children in the parish hall. On weekends the church was a hub of activity and was a popular meeting places that was open to all.

Life in Tafara was full of adventure, learning and deep contentment. One of the first learnings occurred a few weeks after we moved in. We each had a car to travel to our respective ministries and parked them next to the house. We had no gate, no fence – only a hedge between our house and the road. What were we thinking – to put such tantalizing temptation out in the open for all to see? One of the most notorious and well-known thieves in the area jumped at the bait. One morning the white Mazda that Kathryn used was missing. 'Did you give your car to one of the youths to wash?' I innocently asked. Still in her bathrobe and nightgown, Kathryn ran to the road in front of the house shouting: 'Thief! Thief! *Wizi! Wizi!*' Her shouts aroused the neighbors who came running to find out what happened. Within a short time, a posse of men scoured the township looking for a white Mazda. We never expected to see the car again.

A few nights later, a team of youth leaders came to our house with Br Fidelis Mukonori who headed the Youth Department at nearby Silveira House. 'Why didn't you let me know', he asked. 'The youth will find the car'. True to his promise, a few days later the police knocked at our door and asked us to come to identify a white Mazda that had been found and was now at the Motor Vehicles Department when the thief tried to sell the car to a rural teacher. The culprit went to prison for eight years, not for our car but for six others that were found at his property.

'This is the car that came back,' our neighbors said with awe each time they saw it. The car became a symbol of supernatural power that must be protecting us. Kathryn reinforced this perception by nailing a large crucifix to the front of the house next to a picture of the Blessed Mother. I was amused by this appeal to superstition but didn't discourage it. We never again experienced any problem. We also took the added precaution of hiring one of the well-known pickpockets in the neighborhood to help us with cleaning the cars and gardening so that he wouldn't target us in his fundraising exploits and we put up a fence with a gate next to the house to make it a little harder for a car to disappear. We learned that nothing is a secret in the township and that the youth would be our protectors and guides. We also probably earned the reputation as foolish Warungu (foreigners) who didn't know any better and needed to be helped. It was a good way to begin.

With our background in justice and advocacy ministry, it was only natural that we would set up a Justice and Peace Committee in the parish. Fr Path was supportive and encouraged us in this pursuit. About a dozen parishioners joined the committee and we brainstormed where and how to begin. We lobbied our member of Parliament to replace old toilets that were overflowing in the street; we invited representatives of the liberation movements of South Africa and Namibia to address an open air meeting; we set up a St Vincent DePaul Society to provide material assistance to the most needy; we invited the Foreign Minister of Nicaragua, Miguel D'Escoto, who happened to be a Maryknoll priest to address the parish; and we organized a march through the streets of Harare on Africa Freedom Day to support the end of apartheid in South Africa and the release of Nelson Mandela from prison. The march attracted the local media and a front-page photo of Fr Path leading the procession, holding a cross aloft and flanked by youth with placards, caught the attention of the Archbishop. He was not pleased by the publicity and chastised Fr Path for allowing the church to get involved in politics.

Fr Path was not deterred nor were the members of the Committee who were thrilled to make the headlines. Our next endeavor was less rewarding. The Committee decided to take on corruption within the Parish Council. After investigating, they accused the Chairman of stealing money from the weekly collection. He was livid as were the other officers who branded the Committee as power hungry upstarts who wanted to undermine their authority. The Committee never fully recovered from this blow and gradually some members drifted away but we learned the power of advocacy and collective action. We also learned that it is easier to take on injustice outside than to turn the spotlight within. Many years later, members of the parish still refer to the success of the Committee and to the confidence they gained in speaking out and taking action against injustice. It might also be said that the money that had gone missing from the collection returned and some of the guilty members of the Parish Council eventually resigned.

Archbishop Chakaipa came to the parish for confirmations one Sunday. We took the opportunity to invite him to bless our house. He sprinkled every room with holy water and even came outside to sprinkle our garden, toilet and shower. Turning to leave, he said: 'I never thought that white people could live in an African township. You showed me that I was wrong. Thank you for coming here'. With this gracious apology and affirmation of our decision, we never had a problem with the Archbishop.

One of the most painful lessons that we learned was about the treatment of women. While I had witnessed inequality between men and women in Kenya and within my own family when I was growing up in Pittsburgh, I was unaware of the full extent of the injustice until I saw it firsthand among some of our neighbors in Tafara.

The first case to open my eyes happened to our neighbor Rosemary who lived opposite us and enjoyed reading and discussing local and world issues. We looked forward to her visits each week when she came to borrow books from our home library. This intelligent capable woman had a nervous breakdown when her husband impregnated her young sister who had been brought from the rural area to help with the housework and the care of the children. The husband, who worked in a government ministry, sent his wife away and replaced her with her sister. We were shocked and saddened by this injustice. It was the first case of many that we witnessed. Our next-door neighbor, for instance, sent his young wife away when she failed to bear children. He already had several children from a previous marriage but was not satisfied. He threw her out with only her clothes and promptly took another wife who bore him two more children. I was not prepared for the strong grip that culture had on the mentality of both men and women. In Shona culture, a childless union was not a marriage and a woman without a child was an outcast in every way.

We helped the young outcast to get a job and to become financially independent. She eventually married and had two beautiful children but the previous rejection left her scarred for life. The fate of teen-age girls was equally disturbing to me. Several houses down from us lived a family of eight children with a father who cleaned streets and a mother who ran a shebeen to support the family. We tried to find employment for the oldest daughter but eventually her parents sold her to a local policeman who was already married. This young bride suffered beatings from her partner as well as from his first wife who was not happy to share her house and husband with this newcomer. The young bride accepted her fate and bore him two children before she ran away.

Tears flowed freely in our sitting room as women shared their sorrows and disappointments with us. We listened with sadness and dismay as we realized that it would take decades to change these practices and attitudes that discriminated against women. Until women themselves were able to confront them, nothing would change. Much later, I learned from the #MeToo Movement how little had changed throughout the world. This is also a battle that is being waged within the Catholic Church as women advocate for more leadership roles for women, including ordination. While I have never been in the forefront of this movement, I have long felt that the treatment of women is unfair and have grown increasingly impatient with the continuing domination by men in church and society.

When I lived in Tafara, however, such thoughts were far from my mind. There were many happily married couples in our parish and one of our greatest joys was attending weddings. Usually the bride and groom had lived together for many years and had children and grandchildren who accompanied them up the aisle. The church wedding or formalization of the marriage only took place when the man had completed paying the dowry or bride price and when the couple could afford a festive celebration. It was unusual for young people to get married in the church since they did not yet have the funds to afford a proper celebration. However, at least three members of the parish youth group had their weddings when we lived in the township. These were occasions of great rejoicing. The entire parish contributed to support the young couples to have a festive day that they would always remember. I was called upon to ferry the respective brides to the church in my car while Kathryn helped to decorate the hall and prepare the meal.

Such celebrations were part of the fabric of our lives in the township as were the deaths, wakes and funerals. We would learn of a death when neighbors knocked on our door to collect a few dollars or some food for the wake. In the evening we would walk to the home of the deceased and sit on the floor inside the house with the women while the men sat outside in the garden, smoking and drinking locally brewed beer. We sang, danced and prayed with the women until the early hours of the morning when a meal was served. The wake sometimes lasted for several days until all the close relatives arrived, some coming from afar. After the funeral service in the church, all processed to the nearby cemetery where prayers were said and stories shared about the deceased. Kathryn and I joined the mourners to throw a handful of soil into the newly dug grave. Widows often had to be restrained from throwing themselves on top of the coffin and were carried away by attentive friends and relatives. Death felt raw and real, robbing a community and a family of a loved one. Traditional ceremonies were held at the home of the deceased to placate the spirit who it was believed would roam for a year to punish any injustice or ill treatment that he or she had suffered in life. After a year another ceremony was held to put the spirit to rest. The church was aware of these traditions and did not discourage or criticize them. There was an attempt to incorporate some of these rituals into the graveside ceremony but such inculturation was not always a success.

While death among the elders was to be expected, we were puzzled when young people started to fall sick and die. The first that we knew to succumb to a new disease was the young sister of one of the youth leaders who had helped us to move in and was an active member of the Peace and Justice Committee. He asked us to come and pray for his sister who was losing weight and coughing. The local clinic gave her some cough syrup and sent her home. When she failed to improve, Tobias came to the house early one morning and asked me to drive his sister to see the doctor. We carried her to the car as she was too weak to walk. I drove over to the clinic as fast as I could. 'No, no,' Tobias said, 'Not this doctor. I will direct you'. We zigzagged through numerous side streets and stopped at a township house like any other. I planned to wait in the car but Tobias insisted that I come inside.

A young man dressed in a flowing white robe and a feathered headdress welcomed us to a room with several mats on the floor. I was mesmerized as he chanted in a mixture of Latin, Shona and other languages, waving his hands over the young woman and taking several stones from one of her ears. He repeated the gesture and removed feathers from the other ear. He sprinkled water on this pile of stones and feathers and told the girl that her married sister had put a curse on her that he had just removed. 'Arise', he said. She stood and walked out of the house to the car, smiling happily. I couldn't help but think of the miracles of Jesus when he commanded a paralyzed man to get up and walk or when he raised a young girl from the dead.

Dorothy's recovery lasted only a few days, however, before she again lapsed into semi-consciousness. At that time, St Anne's Hospital, run by the Little Company of Mary, had opened a wing for patients with HIV and AIDS with the help of Sally Mugabe, wife of the President. We took Dorothy there and watched as she was gently bathed in warm water, placed in a bed with clean sheets and warm blankets and fed nourishing porridge with peanut butter. This was probably the most luxury she had ever experienced. She revived and lived for another few months. When her condition worsened, she was sent home to die surrounded by her family. We prayed at her bedside as she drew her last breath. Too poor to afford a coffin, the family called the police who placed her tiny body into a large metal box and carried her away.

Tears were all that we could offer as we saw Dorothy take her last breath and then watched her body being carried away. I was not used to being unable to change things for the better and struggled to accept that I was powerless to cure AIDS or to end poverty I finally realized that the most that I could do was to be present to those in pain and to cry with them. I still cry when I remember baby Kathryn, named after my companion Kathryn Shannon. Kathryn was the daughter of Gladys and Charles, a catechist who worked with Sister Kathryn in the parish. Little Kathryn was two years old when she became ill. Her parents took her to the government hospital. When we went to visit, the doctors and nurses were on strike. The nurses left little Kathryn in her bed without food or water. There was a drip at her bedside but they refused to insert it in her arm. As Charles, Gladys, Sr Kathryn and I stood around her bed praying, the baby looked at us with her beautiful big eyes, took a final gasping breath and died. The four of us clung to each other and sobbed while the nurses stood outside in the corridor laughing. Crying was all we could do in the face of such inhumanity and such suffering. A few years later Gladys also died and Charles migrated to South Africa, hoping to begin anew.

After four wonderful years among the people of Tafara, Sr Kathryn was asked to take up a position at our Maryknoll Center in Ossining, NY, and I was winding up my thesis at the University of Zimbabwe and also asked to come back to the States to head our communications office. We departed with much gratitude and a rousing send-off from the people of the parish and the Redemptorist community that had made it possible.

Indeed, the color of our skin mattered to the people of Tafara, not in a negative way as a reminder of colonialism, but in the positive sense that we had access to services, resources and people who could help. We tried to use this power and privilege for the benefit of the people. From the outset we knew that it was not wise to give handouts to individuals as this would only lead to dependence and unending requests. Instead, as mentioned above, we started income-generating projects and a St Vincent de Paul Society to assist the worst cases. We also wrote letters of referral and helped to steer people to the government ministries or organisations that could support them in their particular problem. This was a model that I would follow when I returned again to Zimbabwe seven years later.

23

Disillusion Sets In: Things Fall Apart

Prime Minister Robert Mugabe called me to his office in 1983 a day after the bishops released a statement condemning the vicious military campaign by the North Korean trained Fifth Brigade in Matabeleland and the Midlands. I had never before been called to the Prime Minister's office and was puzzled.

Mugabe greeted me warmly and came straight to the point. 'Why did the bishops not show me the statement first?' He continued, 'I have always been willing to meet them. I learnt about the statement from South African media. If the bishops had come to me, I could have met with the military commanders and intervened. But now I have no choice but to support the commanders.'

I had heard of the statement but not seen it. I was no longer a member of the CCJP and had little contact with the bishops. But I was aware of the rivalry within ZAPU in 1963 that led to the formation of ZANU that same year. I knew that this rivalry continued in subsequent years and sometimes turned violent during the liberation war when their respective armies clashed in areas where both operated. I had witnessed the very different ways that both parties operated during the Lancaster House Conference. In fact, I had interviewed both leaders during this conference for one of the British papers and while each was careful not to criticize or condemn the other, I felt an undercurrent of mistrust and downright hostility.

I should have known better at this point than to take Mugabe at his word. I had witnessed his wrath in 1978 when he received a report that Joshua Nkomo had held secret meetings with Ian Smith in Nigeria. I happened to be in his office with a group of Americans who were touring Mozambique with film-maker and human rights lawyer, Bob van Lierop, when the message came from the Nigerian Ambassador. We held our breath as Mugabe lashed out at the duplicity and hypocrisy of Joshua Nkomo. We turned off our tape recorders and agreed that we would never speak of this incident as we didn't want to contribute to a breakdown in the fragile relations between ZANU and ZAPU which were trying to negotiate together as one 'Patriotic Front'. As more information emerged later about this meeting, it further eroded the little trust that existed between the two movements and solidified the notion that Nkomo was not interested in an alliance between the liberation movements but was willing to go it alone.

In spite of these and other incidents that should have alerted me to the Mugabe's attitude towards ZAPU in general and Joshua Nkomo in particular, I am ashamed to admit I trusted Prime Minister Mugabe and took him at his word. It took me several years before I acknowledged that not only was he aware of what was happening in Matabeleland but had ordered it. I wondered why Mugabe confided in me and what he expected me to do. I think I mumbled something to the effect that he could meet with the bishops and tell them directly what he thought and how this had affected his response. At his next public appearance, Mugabe labeled the bishops 'sanctimonious prelates' and warned them to stay out of politics.

To make up for my ignorance about the bishops' letter, I went to see Bishop Patrick Mutume who was the Secretary General of the Bishops' Conference and a friend. He acknowledged that he and Mike Auret, the National Director of the Justice and Peace Commission, had passed by Prime Minister Mugabe in Parliament the previous day. 'We didn't show him the statement because we believed that he would deny everything and make a counter statement that would be harmful,' Mutume said.

This incident increased the tension between the Catholic Church and the government that had previously welcomed the counsel of the bishops. The Justice and Peace Commission also had the door slammed in its face and its chairman, Mike Auret, was perceived as hostile to the government and as an enemy. I was shaken by this and went to see John Deary, who had chaired the Commission during the war. He and his wife Pat were good friends and I needed to talk to someone about my encounter with Mugabe.

The Dearys were upset by the news. As we talked, we proposed a meeting of the former members of the Justice and Peace Commission and see if there was anything, we could do to bring an end to the violence in Matabeleland and to promote national unity.

About a week later, the Deary's sitting room was the venue for a meeting of Fr Dieter Scholz, Fidelis Mukonori, Ismael and Angela Muvingi, Geoff Feltoe, myself and others. We shared information about the situation in the country and decided that we could use our contacts within both ZANU and ZAPU to advocate for dialogue to end the escalating violence and the divisions that were widening. We prepared a list of talking points and assigned members to meet the various leaders. We approached Ministers Mutumbuka, Zvobgo, Mubako, Nkala and others. Each of the contacts gave us a polite hearing and some of them agreed to urge others in the Party to search for an end to the violence. This was a minor initiative but at least we were trying to do something. Many others were involved in initiatives to bring peace and unity, including President Canaan Banana, who was a Ndebele himself.

Finally, after the loss of at least twenty thousand people and untold suffering, a Unity Accord was signed between Prime Minister Mugabe and Joshua Nkomo in December 1987, bringing an end to the violence and leading to an uneasy truce. Although our intervention had been belated and minor, we were involved and able to use our reputation from the war years to intervene. I never stop believing in the power of individuals to make a difference and the ability of advocacy to bring change.

Land was another issue with deep historical roots going back to the invasion of white settlers in 1890. The inequality in all areas of life was glaringly obvious but the unequal division of the land was one of the most painful to the people. There were stark differences between the fertile land of the white farmers and the parched and barren land left to the local population in 'tribal trust lands.' It could only be a matter of time before these disparities led to revolt and a call for a fairer redistribution.

On my return to the country after Independence, I had an inside view of the land issue through the eyes of Sam Geza, a member of the ZIMFEP Board who was given the responsibility of heading the initial resettlement program. Geza was an intellectual and had joined the liberation struggle. As mentioned earlier, he was accused by leaders in ZANU of being part of a leftist wing within the Party and was arrested and detained in Mozambique for a number of years. He had been married to Mugabe's half-sister with whom he had a son. Geza rejoined ZANU and was given the huge task of implementing a planned program of land reform. I admired Geza's commitment to ending the inequality and felt he had the ability to get the job done. I saw the result of his work on the road to Nyanga and in Gokwe where new farmers were given individual plots. Each resettlement community had a school and a clinic within walking distance. But, for this program to work throughout the country, much patience, and money, was needed.

This program was abruptly shut down in the mid-1980s. No clear explanation was given. There were rumors that the British and the Americans refused to honor the pledge they made at Lancaster House to pay for the reform, that politicians wanted to keep the best land for themselves, that white farmers were needed to keep the economy afloat and reassure donors that Zimbabwe was not a Marxist country. Whatever the true reasons, the land issue smoldered on and led to revolt in the late 1990s.

Land 'invasions' began and intensified under the heat generated by the formation of the Movement for Democratic Change (MDC) in 1999 and the upcoming national elections in 2002. While sympathizing with the motives of the invaders I was concerned they would become violent. Vice-President Simon Muzenda met a group of invaders in Svosve, outside of Marondera, to plead with them to be patient. The government then called on Fr Fidelis Mukonori, a prominent member of the Justice and Peace Commission during the war who had played a part in defusing some of the violence by guerrilla forces. He was well known and respected and able to meet those occupying the land as well as the commercial, mainly white, farmers. While he had some success in the beginning, momentum built up into an apparently unstoppable land grab.

Silveira House Development Training Centre, where I was to work for a number of years, had long run several programs to improve the lives of farm laborers who often lived in crowded and unsanitary compounds on the margins of the commercial land where they labored. The center also ran nutrition improvement programs gave mothers on how to supplement the diet of their children to enable them to grow mentally as well physically. Another program trained community health workers who ran basic health care programs for the workers. The commercial farmers agreed to release one person for at least a day a week to run a clinic on the farm. These health workers, usually women, were given courses in first aid and basic medications to treat common ailments such as colds and flues. I was invited to observe these programs by Thoko Mugwetsi, who was in charge. A member of the administration team at Silveira House, Thoko was very well organized and level headed. The programs were models of efficiency and made a huge difference where they were implemented. But I also gained a first-hand impression of the inequality on the farms and the different attitudes of the commercial farmers. We visited a model farm where the farmer had constructed four-room cottages with electricity for his workers. A neighboring farm was the exact opposite. The pole and thatch houses were dirty and crowded together and there was no sign of a pit latrine in sight. When we met the farmer and suggested the workers could construct pit latrines to provide sanitation, he laughed: 'These people have been going in the bush forever and will continue to do so'. He refused to release one of the workers to gain skills in basic health and nutrition to run a farm clinic.

I wish I knew whether the invaders distinguished between the farmers. Did they take into account how they treated their workers? The murder of David Stevens in April 2000 touched me deeply. I did not know him but he was one of those who treated his laborers with justice and kindness. Although the system itself was unjust and needed to be changed, the murder of individuals was not helping the cause. I later learned that the murderer of Stevens was a former ZIMFEP student who was mentally unstable. I knew him and his brother who was a member of the ZIMFEP staff.

Another incident that affected me personally was the brutal murder of Martin Olds, mentioned earlier, who owned a cattle ranch that bordered George Silundika School in Nyamandlovu. Olds and his wife established cordial relations with the school. Headmaster Matthew Mtobi turned to Olds when the school needed water and Olds often contributed meat to special events at the school while his wife set up the school library. When the farm invasions turned violent, Olds sent his wife, who was in a wheel chair, to Bulawayo for safety. He stayed on the farm and was confronted by an angry group of armed men on 19 April 2000. Outnumbered, Olds was shot on the verandah of his home which was then set on fire. I wrote an impassioned letter to the local media, decrying his death, stating that it undermined the values of the liberation struggle that we were celebrating that day. It was a weak response but all that I could think to do at the time.

As the farm take-overs escalated, Fr Mukonori invited commercial farmers to Silveira House where they would discuss what could be done. On one occasion, I was invited to have tea with Roy Bennett, a well-known farmer from Manicaland and a Member of Parliament. He was also a devout Christian. I recall that he was very cheerful and confident that a solution would be reached without further violence. But the problem had gone on for too long and it was politically expedient to let the invaders have their way. Twenty years later, the country is still dealing with the land issue. Various studies have been done, some showing the benefits to new landholders, especially women, while others pointed to some of the negative consequences of a program that was marred by corruption and cronyism. The plight of the farm laborers, many of whom originated from Malawi and Mozambique, is also largely unknown and under reported. The land issue will continue to plague the country until all parties concerned agree upon a just and equitable arrangement.

Another issue that undermined my relationship with ZANU took place when I was out of the country on home leave in 2005. It was winter in Zimbabwe and the Silveira House Advocacy Program had chosen to focus on urban housing for the poor. We exposed the Members of Parliament to the horrendous living conditions in the so-called informal settlements on the outskirts of Harare. While they were nothing like the slums of Nairobi where some of our sisters and lay missioners worked, places like Dzivarasekwa and Hatcliffe Extensions were not suitable for human habitation. Yet they were growing since there were no other options for those migrating from the rural to urban areas. I began to receive disturbing reports that the army and police were destroying homes and they were forced to flee with the few possessions they could carry. International news media began to broadcast scenes of mass destruction of urban dwellings and the flight of the poor. It is estimated, by a United Nations investigation headed by the head of Habitat, Mrs Anna Tibaijuka, that 700,000 people were made homeless by this action, euphemistically called Operation Murambatsvina, (remove the rubbish). Mrs Tibaijuka was a graduate of Maryknoll schools in Tanzania and well known to our sisters. She briefed us on this mission to Zimbabwe at our regional meeting in Arusha later that year. She told us she requested a private meeting with President Mugabe and told him bluntly what she had observed. She urged him to halt the program before the entire country became under siege. Hers was the first and only first-hand official report and may have played a role in halting further destruction.

When I returned to Harare, I visited some of the Silveira House settlers who had been made homeless. I found those in Hatcliffe Extension living in plastic tents that had been donated by the Redemptorist community that served the people of that area.

24

Knocks on the Door: Silveira House

Father Dieter Scholz, friend and colleague, was Director of Silveira House when I returned to Zimbabwe in 1998 after serving for six years in the Maryknoll Sisters' Communication Department. I went to visit Dieter to catch up on news of Zimbabwe. A few days later, Dieter offered me a job at the Center. I hadn't given a lot of thought about what I would do on my return to Zimbabwe. Silveira House was founded in 1964 at a time of frustration and disillusionment in the nationalist movement. Every country north of the Zambezi was acquiring independence but the white led governments south of the river adamantly refused to share power with the majority of the people, the blacks, indigenous to the region. And to make matters worse the nationalists in Zimbabwe were divided in their stand against the Rhodesian government. Silveira was founded by a Jesuit priest, legendary and beloved John Dove, in an attempt to provide a forum and a training ground to address this frustration and 'wounded dignity', as he called it.

A variety of training programs in both rural and urban areas were developed over the years. The center offered skills training as well as civic education and the training of trade unionists. 'We just answered the knocks on the door', was how John Dove described the growth of the center and became a hub of social and political activity that survived the war years. John, a former soldier in the British army, brought his sense of order and discipline with him when he joined the Jesuits and was assigned to Southern Rhodesia. He would appear to be an unlikely candidate for developing revolutionary training that challenged the British colonial regime.

Unemployed youth also came knocking on John's door, leading to the formation of a dynamic Catholic Youth Movement under the leadership of Jesuit Brother Fidelis Mukonori.[1] It also led to a host of skills training programs for both young men and young women.

I was familiar with the center from my time as a neighbor when I lived in Tafara close by and it had been one of the first places I visited when I came to then Rhodesia in 1977. Fidelis invited me to give a talk to a youth group about life in independent Kenya. John Dove, ever the congenial host, invited me to join the community for a sundowner and a meal after my talk. As we chatted over a gin and tonic and some groundnuts, I was enthralled when John Bradburne, a layman working with people living with leprosy near Mutoko and Dr Luisa Giudotti, doctor at the nearby All Soul's Mission, joined us. Both were working in dangerous areas visited alternatively by the Rhodesian Army and the ZANLA guerrillas. They were good friends of Fr Dove and sometimes came to the center to escape the tension and risks of everyday life in a war zone. I have no idea what we talked about - not the war – but I felt enveloped by a sense of joy and kindness.

After the meal, John and Luisa invited me to go to a film in Harare city center with them. John was wearing sandals, shorts and a cotton shirt while I was shivering in the chill of a Harare

---

1   Fidelis Mukonori is referred to a 'Brother' in this memoir in the earlier sections and 'Father' later. This is simply because he was ordained a priest in 1991.

winter night under several layers of clothing. My need for warmth overrode my desire to spend more time with these two outstanding individuals. I was to meet Luisa at the Justice and Peace Office a few days later but never again met John Bradburne. This one minor incident, however, made a deep impression on me as I felt that I was in the company of very holy people. Luisa was shot and killed by security forces on 6 July 1979 and John was also shot and killed by *mujibas*[2] on 5 September 1979.

So, when Sr Patty Startup, my companion who was the refugee coordinator for southern Africa under the bishops' conferences (IMBISA), encouraged me twenty years later to accept Dieter's invitation to join the staff at Silveira House she was pushing on an open door. My role was to be training director to replace Francis Chirungu, an experienced and long-standing staff member who was retiring. I wondered if I was up to the challenge but accepted with gratitude and excitement.

The decade that I spent at Silveira House (1998 -2008) was a tumultuous period in the history of the country. It coincided with the fast-track land reform, referred to above, and the formation of the Movement for Democratic Change (MDC), a new political party formed by trade unions which would challenge the entrenched position of Mugabe and his party, ZANU-PF. Those years also witnessed the destruction of low income housing in both urban and rural areas, as already mentioned. This cruel program was intended to punish those who voted against ZANU PF in the 2002 elections. The decade also saw hyper-inflation and egregious violence against the opposition MDC. It was not a propitious climate in which to encourage critical thinking – and yet that was the mandate of the center.

In the late 1990s, the center had five departments: Training,

2   *Mujibas* were the 'eyes and ears' of the guerrilla fighters, intermediaries between the fighters and the people. They sometimes took the law into their own hands, as in this case where the guerrilla commander expressly ordered that John be returned to the home where he lived with people with leprosy and not harmed in any way.

193

Rural Development and Agriculture, Research and Publications, internal audit and finance and administration. It was ambitious and offered programs throughout Zimbabwe and in neighboring countries. Training included a commercial school led by Chris Masenyama and a dressmaking program under Evangelista Chakaipa. Aaron Mareya ran appropriate technology and building was led by Jesuit Brother Ladislaus Bvukumbwe. Agnes Mapfumo ran the crafts which included tie and dye and batik fabrics and ran a popular gift shop. In addition, training included Civic Education under the leadership of Ronah Mugadza and Training for Transformation that had been brought from Kenya to Zimbabwe by Anne Hope. Youth and Trade Union courses were also part of training. I interviewed each member of the training staff to find out how they saw their position and what was most important to them. Eventually I joined some of their programs to see for myself the response of the communities that they served and to access the impact they were making.

In this way I visited almost all of Harare Archdiocese, both urban and rural, and became familiar with the various programs and individual staff members. Things were going smoothly during my first year there and I began to relax and enjoy the long overnight trips that involved sleeping on classroom floors, bathing in a tin of cold water and eating *sadza* (maize porridge) and *muriwo* (vegetables). Our regular meetings with our major donor partner, the Misereor representative, Mr Bodo Immink, were generally upbeat and lively.

So, we were taken by surprise when Bodo had to tell us Misereor could no longer support us at the level to which it had hitherto done. 'Funds are shrinking,' he stated plainly. We sat in shocked silence. The Director suggested we needed time to digest this information. The reduction in funding would be 'at least 50%' Bodo told us and he suggested we let go programs now being offered by others, including the Ministry of Education. All heads turned to me. It was obvious that most of the cuts would have to come from the training programs. Bodo reassured us that Misereor would provide retirement packages to those asked to leave.

I was not prepared for this bad news especially since I would have to implement retrenchments of people I was still getting to know. I tried to put a positive spin on the lay-offs at the farewell parties we held for departing staff. But the individuals who would be out of a job in a few months were disappointed and even angry. Inflation began to escalate at the very time their packages were given to them and the real value of what they received was greatly diminished.

I also tried another tack. I had the experience of setting up production units in ZIMFEP – self-reliant, income-generating projects. I suggested that the craft unit could easily become self-reliant. Already the Art Peace Cooperative stone-carving group that was based at Silveira House was independent and the members seemed to be earning enough to support themselves and their families. The craft unit agreed and looked for ways to earn additional income.

The Commercial School and Dressmaking Program found a new home at the Young Africa Center in Chitungwiza that was initiated by Raj and Dorien Beurskens, a dynamic couple who had done something similar in Kenya. Young Africa programs linked skills training with business studies and values education, a holistic program that enabled graduates to run their own enterprises. The model seemed to work and we rejoiced that the programs did not have to close but could simply migrate.

Two of the original programs, for trade unions and the youth, simply ceased. Most unions now had their own training schemes and our training had shifted focus to workers' committees, imparting information about legislation. 'Are we helping management rather than improving the lives of the workers?' our staff asked. We knew any challenge to the program would be resisted and asked our Research Unit to evaluate the program. The results were even worse than we expected. The research included the staff of the program so they had to accept the results, even if reluctantly. We retrenched the two staff members who went on to work as independent trainers.

The Youth Program was even more problematic. Our four trainers were well known and liked throughout the Archdiocese and yet the program had changed little over the years and new models were emerging throughout the country. Again, we called on the Research Unit to conduct an evaluation. The results were so negative that the trainers threatened to sue us. Eventually they accepted the generous retirement packages but it left me feeling exhausted and depressed.

But we bounced back and initiated two new programs within the training section that raised my spirits. Peace Building emerged in response to the increased violence in the country. In his research for the Zimbabwe bishops' conference, Ranga Zinyemba had identified the Center for Conflict Resolution (CCR) in Cape Town as one of the best training programs on the continent. I met the training director when I was in Cape Town for another meeting and explained our situation. The response was instant and positive. The Center would send us two of their best trainers over a period of two years to give us specialized courses to meet our needs. We would use a participatory methodology much like the one that we used in our civic education and Training for Transformation courses. Thus, began a long and fruitful relationship with CCR and with Val Dovey, their youth trainer. Val came to Silveira House every few months with different colleagues to train us in each phase of the program, including mediation and negotiation skills as well as an introduction to conflict resolution. Val was energetic, creative and made learning fun.

We did role plays and case studies and were soon able to go out into communities to mediate local conflicts that were often domestic disputes or quarrels over animals that were destroying crops. It was during the time of the land invasions and in one of the role-plays we had Sr Scholastica, a sister on the staff, take the part of a landless peasant and Cuthbert Chamboko, took the part of the commercial farmer. After a heated discussion, the two changed sides. Scholastica was now the farmer and Cuthbert the landless peasant. Now they saw the issue from the other side and were able to reach a compromise! 'You can keep half of the land and the farmhouse. I will take the other half and the barn. We will share the tractor and other farm machinery,' the peasant farmer suggested. The commercial farmer agreed but insisted, 'Let us sign a letter of agreement and have it approved by the District Administrator. This will protect both of us when others want to claim the land.'

This was 'make believe' but it gave us a sense of how to dialog and reach a compromise. We learned to analyze a conflict and recognize the needs, interests and values of each of the parties. We began to test our skills with local communities. One session will always stand out for me. A war veteran stood up at the end of the workshop and declared: 'I have told my wife to hide my gun. I don't need it anymore. Now I know that I can resolve conflicts with words,' Not all our sessions were so successful. During one workshop the group split in two with half of the war veterans refusing to participate. The others used their skills to reach a consensus that those not interested could leave but that the rest would remain.

One of the worst cases happened in our own backyard. The people of Chishawasha invited us to give them a Peace Building Workshop. As was the custom, they contributed food for the meals and firewood. We had only finished introductions when a group of youth entered the hall. 'We will burn down the hall and your vehicles if you don't leave,' they told the trainers. One of the invaders was heard to say, 'if we let you stay you will open the eyes of the people and they won't vote for us anymore.' With this rare admission of the value of the training, the trainers left rather than risk damage to the hall and the vehicles. A few weeks later, a delegation came from the Valley to apologize for not standing up to the invaders and inviting us back.

We also used our skills with the police and with local government officials. The program was accepted and was spreading throughout the country. As violence continued to escalate other organisations embarked on peace building and conflict resolution. We collaborated as much as possible.

Another new program that met the needs of the time was Advocacy. At one of our monthly planning sessions, Ronah Mugadza and I responded to an advert in the local paper for an advocacy program funded by USAID. Ronah, one of our most experienced and dynamic trainers, identified three areas that she thought would fit the criteria: sustainable use of wetlands could be incorporated in the Silveira House agriculture program. The issue could be included in environmental legislation that was soon to be introduced to Parliament: A second issue was the provision of low-income housing for the homeless, using our programs in the squatter communities in Dzivaresekwa and Hatcliffe Extensions. The third issue involved our relationship with the Justice and Peace Commission in Binga with whom we had recently published and launched a book: *The People of the Great River*. The launch convinced us that we could collaborate on other issues as well such as skills training for women and youth.

When we approached Fanuel Cumanzala, the Coordinator of Binga Justice and Peace, he responded enthusiastically and we found ourselves making the long and tiring journey to Binga in the Zambezi valley. The Tonga is a matrilineal society. Inheritance passes through the woman and her husband moves to her compound and becomes part of her family rather than the other way around. It also means that women are very outspoken and take leadership roles in the community. The British imposed male chiefs in the area but women are powerful and make most of the local decisions. Looked at through my white American prism, I found the Tongo full of good humor in spite of their oppressed background. They are creative and courageous, eager to stand up and speak to members of Parliament. Although many of the members of the language committee were men, we knew that at home if the women did not support the issue it did not pass. We found the male chiefs open to dialog and ready to listen to their constituents. I had a reputation among Silveira House staff for 'over praising'. I suspect that I would earn that title in this case.

Hundreds of people gathered at Binga to meet us and tell us their issues. They used a process that allowed each person to speak and to enroll others to their cause. By the time we arrived the community was united around one common issue. On the long drive to Binga we had thought destruction to their crops caused by elephants would be an issue and, in preparation, we had studied how other communities had deterred elephants in humane ways, such as making fences from plants that attracted bees. Another suggestion was regaining access to their ancestral right to fish in the lake as they used to. I pondered what lawyer would work on this with us. I was excited as we gathered to listen to the spokespersons. One after another rose and spoke eloquently; 'Our children can't speak to their grandparents,' a respected woman in the community said. 'They need to learn their own language in school.' One speaker after another stressed the need to teach Tonga in schools in the district where the Tonga were the dominant group. The speakers became more animated as the discussion continued: 'We dream in our own language,' a village elder added. 'We pray in our own language,' a senior chief said eloquently. 'But we can't speak to our grandchildren in our language.'

It was clear that we, from Harare, had no idea what really mattered to the people of Binga. Yes, fishing rights were important and so was the control of elephants but what mattered most to the majority of the people we met was preserving their language and culture. Fanual was amused at our incomprehension. It was the classic case of outsiders with good intentions coming to build a school or a clinic when what the community wanted was a sports field. We were fortunate that our hosts would take the lead with this program. Fanual hired a local teacher, Isaac Mumpande, to conduct research on what languages were being taught in this predominantly Tonga area. We launched his research findings at a meeting in the open air that was attended by headmasters, teachers, education officers and members of Parliament. The research was unbiased and showed a depressing pattern of the Ndebele language being taught in most of the schools in the district rather than Tonga. Even in the first three grades where indigenous languages may be taught, this was not the case in Binga.

Isaac made his case eloquently and clearly. It led to a resolution to take the matter to Parliament with an emphasis on training teachers and sourcing teaching materials in the Tonga language. Zambia was already using Tonga in its schools and so we initially used books from Zambia. Tisa Chifunyisa who was working with Save the Children at the time was a great help in securing teaching material. Her commitment to the cause eventually took her life as she died from malaria after one of those trips. She will always be remembered as one of the pioneers in promoting local languages.

Isaac and Fanual realized the power in numbers. The Tonga

were not the only marginalized group in Zimbabwe. If they could win over others – the Nambya, Sotho, Venda, Shangaan and others who spoke minority languages -, they would speak with a louder voice. Indigenous language groups were formed and became active. They could not be ignored. It took five years of lobbying Parliament and holding meetings with local communities to have a Bill passed in Parliament for the teaching of indigenous languages up to Grade 7 in schools where a particular group were the majority. The focus moved to the Constitution that was being debated throughout the country. It was about another ten years before the Constitution was approved with a section on language, which recognized the rights of all the people of Zimbabwe to have their language taught in schools to their children.

As the years passed, I was completely at home at Silveira House. On a purely personal level when there were food shortages in the country, I could buy milk at the dairy, clean water from the borehole, chickens from the women's group and vegetables from the garden – what a bounty that I could share with neighbors. For other things we had to join any queue that materialized, knowing that we probably needed whatever was being offered. Once when we got to the front of the queue, we were given a box of matches. A loaf of bread might have been more welcome but we each took the matches with gratitude since we needed them to light candles at night with all the power cuts.

About three quarters through my ten-year term at Silveira House, I decided that it was long past time to hand over my position to a local person. Our Maryknoll philosophy was that we were only there for a while and should hand over to local leadership as soon as possible. After discussions among the management committee, Mr Ignatius Musona was chosen as the new Training Director. Ignatius had joined us as a teacher from Chinhoyi to work in the Advocacy Program. He came a day late for the interview and I was tempted to send him away but was convinced by his interest in the position and his open and humorous attitude. It turned out that he had only seen the advert that very day. 'I immediately jumped on a bus to Harare to arrive early and be one of the first in the queue for the post.'

Ignatius joined the Advocacy Program and was active in all three of the issues: environmental, urban development and language and culture. He gained experience in addressing communities, drafting legislations and speaking to Members of Parliament. He worked well with others on the team and I was happy to turn over my leadership portfolio to him and to step into the Research and Publications Department that was always my first love.

We had lost Munhumeso Manenji, one of the best local researchers that we would ever have, in a tragic motor bike accident on his way home. Manenji was politically astute and gave me a rare insight into the thinking of the 'born frees', those born after Independence who had no experience of colonial Rhodesia and the violence of the war. They were skeptical of high-sounding rhetoric that was not followed through with action. As living standards in the country dropped and political violence increased, they were eager and ready for change. I had a tendency to follow the government media and to accept the official party line. Little by little, Manenji and other youth opened my eyes to the lies that I was being fed daily and they helped me to see that there might be other better solutions to the problems that the country faced.

Although I continued to attend the wakes and funerals of war veterans who I had known and respected and to attend National Holiday celebrations, I began to seek out lectures and articles by members of the opposition. I found that most of their facts were correct and that their analysis of what had gone wrong in the country since Independence were sound and well argued.

I referred earlier to our research unit. Silveira House had set this up in the 1990s with a particular emphasis on studying the impact of the Economic Structural Adjustment Program (ESAP). Policy choices by the new government after independence led to a virtual collapse of the agricultural, mining and manufacturing sectors that had made Zimbabwe a relatively prosperous country in the past. By the 1990s the World Bank and the IMF demanded 'adjustments' as the price of further financial support. These changes failed to produce good results; the number of those in formal employment fell drastically and the people relied on informal self- employment and vending.

Two Jesuits at Silveira House, Peter Balleis and Brian MacGarry, produced a series of booklets outlining the deteriorating impact of ESAP. The unit they established was still flourishing under new management when I arrived in 1998.

My own work on the liberation war had just been published as I was joining Silveira House. It appeared under the title, *On the Frontline, Catholic Missions in Zimbabwe's Liberation War*,[3] and was perhaps unusual in that it was the fruit not only of my research, focusing on four Catholic missions, but of my experience in the war. Smangaliso Mkhatshwa, Deputy Minister of Education in the new majority rule government of Nelson Mandela and a Catholic priest, wrote in the foreword, 'the Churches (in South Africa and Zimbabwe) were active participants in the colonial enterprise and in its eventual demise. This volume documents how the Catholic Church made this transformation and goes on to describe the interaction between guerrillas and Church personnel at four rural missions. (It) raises critical issues of morality and ethics, throwing light on the complex subject of religion and politics and highlighting changes in church-state relations over the years.'

Like so many people at the turn of the new century I was

---

3   Baobab Books: Harare. 1996.

struggling to understand what went wrong. Why did the dream die? Julius Nyerere had told Robert Mugabe that he had inherited a jewel and added, 'Make sure you keep it that way', or words to that effect. Mugabe did not carry out this advice. Many of our studies, in the research unit at Silveira House revolved around this issue, though we did not restrict ourselves to it. We produced a collection of papers under the title, *Zimbabwe, the Past is the Future,* and I was involved in soliciting many of them. As Arkmore Kori, who headed the Research Program after the tragic death of Manenji put it, 'those affected by the social and economic policies resulting from ESAP – and the pandemic of HIV and AIDS – cried but were not heard'. Kori went on, 'and they expected more than a deep understanding of their issues. They wanted action by the policy makers.' In other words, our research had to be 'action-oriented'. We were building, Kori acknowledged, on the tradition of round table discussions started by Fr John Dove in 1964. Our aim was, 'National Dialogues and engaging with policy makers on issues raised in our research.'

Our 'Silveira House Social Series' publications put the voices of the poor on record and were distributed through a network of development partners, the media, book shops and reviews. The demand was for what became the 'Research, Advocacy and Publications Department' to also become a 'service' department. It carried out needs assessments, monitored ongoing programs and evaluated those that had ended. It was a strategic mix: speaking for the voiceless and providing real time, faith and evidence-based programming information.

25

Losing My Freedom: Accepting the Responsibility of Congregational Leadership

'How does it feel to be the President of the Maryknoll Sisters?' asked Salim Salim, Tanzania's former Ambassador to the United Nations and the former Secretary General of the Organisation of African Union. He answered his own question: 'You lose your freedom.' I realized that he was speaking from his own experience and that it summed up mine as well. If you truly listen to the views of others and respond to their needs, you give up a part of yourself. It can be painful but it is also liberating.

I had reluctantly left my name in when I was nominated to leadership at our General Assembly in 2008. At previous assemblies I had expressed my regrets as I stepped down, feeling inadequate and unworthy for such a post. As I approached my 70s, however, I realized that it might be time to be open to this huge responsibility. I had received so much from the congregation that I loved. Maybe now it was time for me to give back. I was not surprised when elected since I was well known. I had interviewed many of our members for articles in the Maryknoll magazine. My arrest and deportation from white-ruled Rhodesia had also added to the myths surrounding me – that I was strong, capable and courageous; a creative thinker who could help bring change to our community. Little did they know that this was only the outward image that I projected while I was extremely traditional in many ways and not likely to rock the boat. I was especially conscious of the feelings and views of our senior members who were now retired and who I felt deserved our respect and understanding.

Three women were then elected as members of the leadership team. Rebecca Macugay from the Philippines who had worked in Kenya, Namibia and South Africa, was chosen as the Vice-President. Ann Hayden, a nurse from Kentucky who had worked in Korea and Nicaragua, was elected as a member of the Council as was Bitrina Kirway, a younger member from Tanzania who was working with indigenous communities in Hawaii. They were creative, intelligent, hard-working and lots of fun but we didn't yet know each other.

One of the problems with a far-flung community such as ours is that our paths seldom cross except when we return for renewal every few years or if we reside in the same region or entered together in the same year. The four of us newly elected to leadership came from different backgrounds and had never worked together. I barely knew Ann and Bitrina but had interacted with Becky when we were both members of the Kenya Region. We, therefore, hired a facilitator to start us off with team building. Without this first step in getting to know each other at deeper levels and in learning our different styles of operating, it might have taken us much longer to reach consensus on tough issues or to work together compatibly in spite of not always agreeing.

A few days after we were in office, I visited former President,

Barbara Hendricks, in our nursing home. She had steered us through the confusing years after Vatican II when many sisters were leaving the community and much that we had known and accepted was now being questioned. Her visionary leadership kept us united and moved us to adopt an option for the poor and to embrace liberation theology. Her personal friendship with many of the liberation theologians that she had known in Peru gave us a firm footing and a clear direction for the future. She had sent me to Rhodesia and welcomed me back when I was deported in 1977.

Barbara was now incapacitated and seldom spoke or interacted with others. When I greeted her, thanked her for her leadership and asked her for advice, she looked straight at me and said: 'Go out to the regions as soon as you can. That's where you will see firsthand what we are about.' The following words still ring in my heart: 'Trust the sisters,' she said. 'They have great wisdom and will teach you what to do.' With that endorsement, I felt a sense of peace and let go of my insecurity and fear. These visits were indeed eye-opening and encouraging. At that time, our members were spread over 24 regions or countries. The four of us divided up this enormous outreach and travelled at least once in our term to each of the regions to which we were liaisons.

Our first big challenge came at the beginning of 2009. Less than a month into our term of office we received a letter from the Vatican Secretariat for Religious informing us of an 'Apostolic Visitation' of religious communities of women in the United States. The purported rationale for such an exercise was to find out the reasons for the decline in religious vocations. Unwritten but understood was the less benign intention of critiquing the changes that had taken place in religious life as a result of the Second Vatican Council. There were those who believed that if we returned to the former more institutionalized way of life, put on habits and adopted a semi-cloistered existence behind convent walls that young women would flock to join us.

After consulting canon lawyers and receiving helpful advice from the Leadership Conference for Women Religious (LCWR), we dutifully filled out all the forms that were submitted to us and prepared to receive a team of three visitors. I personally never had a doubt that our way of life would be vindicated and our mission charism endorsed. At a meeting to inform our sisters at the center of this exercise, the four of us on the leadership team assured the members that we had nothing to fear from this process. 'We are proud of who we are', I recall saying to them. More than eighty of our sisters agreed to be interviewed by the three visitors who were very open and interested in who we are and how we carry out our mission.

We agreed to show the same hospitality to these visitors as we would to any others but we were unanimous in stating that we would not pay for their visit. Our team used this opportunity to model a participatory form of leadership in which we invited others to prepare a welcoming service and to accompany the visitors as they carried out their mandate. We prepared an overview of our Constitution and of our membership and mission outreach but in every other way, we involved the members at the center to look after and guide the visitors.

In hindsight, the 'Apostolic Visitation' was a blessing in disguise since it helped us to define our identity as a mission congregation, to develop knowledge of our Constitutions and to articulate the vision of our founder, Mother Mary Joseph. In the next few years, we accompanied the LCWR as it faced the challenge of an investigation into its very existence. The LCWR informed and consulted its more than 900 members every step of the way and adopted contemplative dialog as the method for making decisions. I marveled at the ability of the LCWR leadership team to maintain a positive outlook and a non-violent approach to the constant

grilling by officials in Vatican offices, some of whom were hostile ·
to the organization. Some of the opposition seemed to come
from a clash of cultures between American values of freedom and
maturity and Italian notions of hierarchy and obedience.

The report of the visitation that we received after leaving office
was overwhelmingly positive. The questions that it raised about
our training program for new members were questions that we
ourselves were asking. The concern for our financial sustainability
in view of many aging members requiring long-term care was also
the concern of our financial advisors. We, therefore, were not
disappointed by the report and felt vindicated by its conclusions.

Caring for the health of our members, especially our seniors,
was one of the major challenges that we faced given the high cost
of health care in the United States. Our congregation had no health
insurance policy and would soon run out of funds if we continued
as we were at the time. We had heard of some innovative programs
for women religious on the West Coast and set up a team to
investigate options. Sisters Ellen McDonald, Dolores Congdon
and Sue Baldus were tireless in finding out what was available
and preparing reports that were sent to all our members. We also
invited two former members of our congregation who had helped
to set up Medicare and Medicaid programs for the government to
join us. Lillian Gibbons and Regina McPhillips added first hand
expertise to the project as did Sr Geraldine Brake, then coordinator
of our health program for our seniors.

Fortuitously, at the same time the Administration of President
Barak Obama was exploring ways to make health care more
affordable and accessible to all. The Archdiocese of New York
was doing the same. These initiatives intersected in Archcare, a
program under the Archdiocese of New York to lower the costs of
health care for their religious personnel. Maryknoll Sisters around
the world voted on which model we would adopt, given several

options. With the input from our members, we chose to adopt a Managed Long Term Care program under Archcare that would enable us to obtain Medicaid as well as Medicare assistance from the government.

The choice was not unanimous and emotions ran high. I trusted the wisdom of our members who had written in their views but I felt the anger of some sisters, including a few with whom I had been close. As I grappled with my own feelings of failure, I recalled the words of a bishop in Zimbabwe when I was writing my doctoral thesis. 'If some people don't criticize you, you won't have done anything.' Each time our team made hard decisions; these words of Bishop Patrick Mutume gave me strength. I don't like being unpopular but I realized that pleasing everyone was not possible nor was it a good thing to try and do.

The hundredth anniversary of our congregation came in the middle of our term of office and was one of the highpoints of our six years in leadership. Various events were planned for 2012, both at our Center and in our mission regions. The hard work and creativity of the members who were planning each event was very inspiring and reassuring. I only had to show up and say a few words of welcome at most of these occasions that had been meticulously orchestrated by various teams that included former members, graduates of our schools and sisters with enthusiasm and organizational ability.

Relatives of Mary Josephine (Mollie) Rogers, our founder, came to the opening ceremony at our center on the Feast of the Epiphany, the day on which the first three women had arrived in 1912, the nucleus of the first community of Catholic women devoted to mission in the United States. They only became religious in 1920 when their numbers had grown and it seemed that this was the only route to go to China as missioners. Timothy Dolan, Archbishop of New York, was the celebrant at the Mass. I was able to be among the first to congratulate him for being named a Cardinal the previous day. He had grown up not far from our novitiate in Valley Park, Missouri, so had a soft spot for Maryknoll Sisters.

Coincidentally, three visitors from Zimbabwe arrived that weekend and added to the festivities by bringing a huge cake, bottles of champagne for each table and colorful balloons. Sr Irene Rufaro, LCBL, was one of the first people whose case I covered for the CCJP when she was detained in a small rural town. Her friends, Angie and Gladys Taderera, had worked for the World Bank and the International Monetary Fund (IMF) respectively and their family was well known for its support of the liberation struggle.

In the back of my mind throughout the celebration was the knowledge that my sister Mary Ellen was hosting her annual New Year's celebration in the nursing home where she was resting after collapsing at her home in Brooklyn on Thanksgiving Day. Since she could not go home, she invited her friends to come to her. Her spirit of perseverance amazed me. I had been with her when she collapsed and had seen her struggling to breath since then. She had given me good suggestions for the opening talk that I gave at the Mass. She was never far from me.

Early in our six-year term, the four of us agreed that we needed expert advice in areas where we lacked knowledge and experience and areas that we believed were critical for the future of the congregation I was given the task to develop guidelines for such an advisory board while all of us submitted names of people we thought could assist us. We agreed that we needed advice in the fields of media, finance, environment and international trends and chose Mark Edmiston, Dan Neuman, Sr Chris OP, and Carolyn Woo, respectively.

To me, this was an inspired decision and one of the most

enjoyable and rewarding of our many initiatives. We openly shared our concerns and the reality of our congregation with kindred spirits who were in tune with us. They gave us very helpful advice and provided support and solidarity when we most needed it. Our quarterly meetings became times of spiritual enrichment and mutual support and encouragement. When Carolyn Woo took on the demanding task of heading Catholic Relief Services, Marie Dennis, co-President of Pax Christi International and former head of the Maryknoll Office of Global Concerns replaced her. Carolyn remained a good friend and supporter and often sent us helpful advice and information and Marie provided continuity and new insights into global trends.

My first invitation to our regions overseas was from our sisters in Japan who asked me to attend an inter-religious dialog on Japanese Buddhism. 'This is the best way for you to learn about the culture,' our sisters in Japan said. They were so right. We visited Buddhist temples and Shinto shrines and spent the night in a famous temple on Mount Fuji and woke early in the morning for the Kitaguchi Hongu Fuji Sengen Shrine fire ceremony.

The highlight of those six years was the induction of our founder into the Women's Hall of Fame in Seneca Falls, NY. We had submitted her name on several occasions and finally in 2014 we received a positive response. I was expected to give the ten-minute talk at the ceremony and called together a group of our sisters to brainstorm as was my habit when asked to give a major address. I practiced my delivery with several sisters who gave me positive feedback and felt confident when I faced a crowd of several hundred, including relatives of Mother Mary Joseph who we had invited. Our founder was one of several women being inducted at that ceremony. I was placed between Kate Millet, a well-known feminist writer, and Nancy Pelosi, Democratic politician who would become the Speaker of the House. Coincidentally, Nancy's husband had roomed with my cousin at Lehigh University and they formed a successful business together. In addition to her Catholic background, therefore, Nancy and I bonded over this relationship. When I finished my short speech, Nancy gave me a thumbs up that made me feel as if I could run for the US Congress!

I sum up those grueling but rewarding six years with what one senior sister dubbed 'the three Ps' – pastoral, prophetic and public. Our Constitutions are very clear that the President is meant to unify. I made my main aim to be present to each and every member; to listen to their concerns, to visit the sick, to pray with the dying and to encourage the young and those in difficulty. I treasure the time spent with each member and regret that there were others with whom I rarely interacted.

At our first training with LCWR for new leaders we were advised to give eighty per cent of our time to mission and twenty to problem-solving. This was an ideal that I often neglected as some of the individual needs took up an inordinate amount of time. Although my secretary did her best to schedule appointments, I sometimes overrode her good intentions and let individuals see me whenever they wished. Although I often left exhausted from these encounters, I do not regret these choices, similar to those I have made overseas when people were in need. I often say that people will not remember how many schools that I helped to build or how many journalists I trained but they will recall that I visited a sick relative in the hospital or attended the funeral of a loved one. I am convinced that it is these personal pastoral acts of compassion and caring that stand out and mark us as followers of Jesus.

Having taken a stand for justice most of my life, it was not surprising that I was given the portfolio of the Maryknoll Office for Global Concerns (MOGC). This was a collaborative initiative of all three Maryknoll entities (sisters, fathers and brothers) and represented us at the United Nations and in the halls of Congress.

The Office issued public statements in the name of Maryknoll and our lay missioners and advocated on issues we were engaged in.

We faced a crisis halfway through our term when the Director of the office resigned for personal reasons. Marie Dennis was the heart and soul of the office for twelve years and we didn't see how we could replace her. We asked her deputy to take over and, when she declined, we did a major search. After many false starts, we hired a former lay missioner who had lived in Venezuela with his wife and two daughters and then had served in leadership with the lay missioners. He understood mission as well as the complex relations between the three branches of Maryknoll and turned out to be just what was needed at the time to bring stability and encouragement to the staff who were fearing that the whole enterprise would collapse.

A public role was expected of whoever was elected to serve as President. It was a familiar role to me as I had joined the debating team in high school and learned to speak before an audience and to improvise on the spur of the moment. I had gained experience in testifying before Congress from my early days in Maryknoll and had learned to speak before a microphone and a camera when I studied communications at Marquette University. When I was deported from Rhodesia, I became an overnight sensation and was interviewed endlessly in Europe as well as in the States. I enjoyed being in the limelight and could think on my feet. I was asked to give the keynote address at the US Catholic Mission Association Conference (USCMA). Maryknoll missioners had been instrumental in forming this organization that was intended to awaken a missionary spirit among Catholics in the States. When the invitation came from the Director of USCMA, Fr Michael Montoya, I hemmed and hawed and tried to get out of it. 'Just tell your story,' Michael said. 'You don't need to give a theological treatise or a high-flown speech. Just be yourself. You have a lot to share.' With this encouragement, I agreed and worked on my talk for several weeks. I used this opportunity to share some of the lessons that I had learned as well as to highlight the changes that were occurring in the church and the world that necessitated a new way of being in mission. I learned later that the head of the Propagation of the Faith in the States who was present called my speech 'fluff'. I had tried to reach a large lay audience by being down to earth and using real-life examples. It seems that I succeeded!

I served on several boards and received two honorary degrees – one from Marquette, my alma mater, and one from Albertus Magnus College in New Haven, Connecticut, my sister's alma mater. I knew that the honor belonged to our congregation and not to me personally. I recalled the words of Sr Maria del Rey when she asked sisters to give interviews and to appear on radio and TV. 'This is for Maryknoll,' she explained. 'It's not about you.' My favorite recognition came at the end of my six years in leadership as the Thomas Merton Center in Pittsburgh nominated me as 'A Distinguished Daughter of Pennsylvania'. I had lived far away from Pennsylvania for more than fifty years, but I was proud to come from Pittsburgh and excited to be listed among other well-known women from Pennsylvania. The three other members of our team accompanied me to Harrisburg, the State capital, where the Governor and his wife presented the awards.

When the six years in leadership were over, I breathed a huge sigh of relief. I was glad that I had accepted this great responsibility and even more glad that I could hand it on to others. It was a crash course in learning about our community and also learning about other religious communities. I came to appreciate that most religious were as deeply committed to justice as Maryknoll Sisters and equally heroic in their service to the poor and vulnerable. I came to see the dark side of the institutional church but also met many saintly people within its ranks. But most of all I learned about myself. I discovered that I was much happier being a gadfly on the margins, a maverick and often a pain to those in leadership. When it was my turn to be in the hot seat, it brought out the traditional side of me, the side that grew up in the pre-Vatican II church and still admired many of the old customs and traditions. I discovered to my surprise that I didn't want to rock the boat and was happy to preserve the trappings of the past. The three wise women who served with me often pulled me out of my comfort zone as did my friends and relatives, especially my sister, who challenged me to take risks and to be unconventional.

Leadership also brought out a royalist streak in me that enjoyed the pomp and ceremony of office as well as the perks. Meeting with bishops and papal nuncios was fun and speaking before an audience gave me energy. My sister pricked my balloon on many occasions and helped me to laugh at myself and my pretensions. After a joyous liturgical celebration over which I presided when all and sundry greeted and thanked me, one of our sisters came up and whispered in my ear. I thought she had some private words of praise to share. 'You should stand up straight,' she said, 'or you will have a permanent hump in your back'. After I recovered from surprise, I laughed. Her words were an echo of my mother's constant refrain as I was growing up. I was tall for my age and tended to stoop or bend over so I would fit in with others. It was a good lesson in humility and I often think of it when I'm tempted to overrate myself.

26

You Don't Understand:
Facing My Sister's Death

I grew up believing that I had power to influence life and to protect and rescue others, especially Mary Ellen, my little sister by three years. We were only two in the family and were close. She had curly red hair – not gaudy fire engine red but a rich mahogany hue - and dark brown eyes. I thought that she was the most beautiful person I had ever seen.

I was tall and thin with a long face and nose like my father's. I thought that I was ugly but smart. I used my brain to succeed in life. Mary Ellen was also smart but had to follow in my footsteps. I learned much later that she asked my parents not to send her to a college where I had been. Apparently, the Dominican Sisters who taught us always asked her why she couldn't be more like her sister. With this incentive pushing her, she went to Albertus Magnus College instead of St Mary of the Springs in Columbus, Ohio, where I had gone for a year before joining Maryknoll.

She did her degree in social work and went on to get her Masters at Fordham while working at Angel Guardian Home in Brooklyn, which specialized in foster care and adoption. She spent the next 42 years championing the rights of children. She led the merger of McMahon Services for Children with Good Shepherd and served as co-director with Sr Paulette LoMonaco, who became a trusted colleague and friend. Together they expanded the agency and spearheaded several creative initiatives to support children at risk and to strengthen their family network.

Although I lived thousands of miles away, first in Kenya and then in Zimbabwe, we reconnected instantly when I returned to the States for my periodic renewal program. We seemed able to read each other's minds and didn't have to explain much. One of the benefits of my election as president of our community was that I would be closer to Mary Ellen and her husband, Barrett Mansfield. For six years. I enjoyed the train ride down the Hudson River and the subway ride from Grand Central Station to downtown Brooklyn where I walked the few blocks to their apartment on Atlantic Avenue to spend enjoyable weekends with them.

Mary Ellen and I inevitably went shopping, one of her favorite past-times. She enjoyed replacing my old clothing with more modern outfits. Sometimes we would go to the Brooklyn Botanical Gardens where Barrett volunteered or to a film and to a nearby restaurant for a meal. I savored these moments together when we would talk about anything and everything. We shared similar views about the world and were especially vocal about injustice of any kind. We both worked with the poor and marginalized and knew firsthand the hurdles they had to overcome to get ahead in life. We realized the advantages that we had received as white, middle class Americans with well-educated and wealthy relatives. We knew that we were among a small privileged minority among the world's population and felt an obligation to pass it on by empowering the less fortunate.

We made plans while I was in the States to do things together as she did with her friends. We would go to Weston Abbey in Vermont for Holy Week, join the Pax Christi trip to protest at the School of the Americas in Georgia, and go on a vacation to Scotland and Wales. She invited me to speak at St Barnabas parish about my work and to join her Pax Christi group for their monthly meetings. We were making up for lost time when our worlds fell apart. It started with an operation for cancer under her left arm and progressed to a hacking cough that wouldn't go away. After endless visits to various doctors, she was diagnosed with pneumonitis, a lung disease of no known cause. 'Perhaps some environmental poisoning', the doctors said. It was irreversible, progressive and fatal. I was unwilling to accept this diagnosis and kept looking for cures. 'Maybe if you move out of the city, your lungs will improve. Maybe you should get another opinion. Maybe you can get a lung transplant'. I offered her a lung. She laughed and said, 'I think I need two'. 'One is better than none', I countered.

With each suggestion, she looked and me and sighed, 'You don't understand'. She was right. She was dying slowly, day by day, and I refused to accept defeat. She was my little sister. Surely, I could find a cure that all the best lung specialists had missed! By the beginning of 2011, she was carrying a small oxygen tank with her to work. She continued to take the long subway ride from Brooklyn to the Bronx and rarely took a day off from work. For her it was a vocation, not a job. When she turned 65 on July 25, 2011, she finally left this work that gave her such satisfaction. I treasured the words of praise that her colleagues showered upon her at her retirement party and told them that she was the missionary at home while I worked abroad. I assured them that hers was the much more difficult vocation and deserved more praise than mine.

Not long after that, she sent me off to South Sudan to volunteer for a month. It was my gift for my Golden Jubilee. I had asked her if she wanted to go to Ireland with me to find our roots. 'You must be joking', she said. 'You should do something meaningful to celebrate your fifty years in Maryknoll, something that will witness to the purpose of your lifelong commitment to justice'. I was disappointed as I wanted to learn more about my Irish ancestors but I gave her suggestion serious thought. South Sudan had just achieved independence after decades of war. Maryknoll Sisters had served there throughout the long years of war between North and South as well as the internal fighting that pitted one tribe against another. 'What about giving peace building training in South Sudan', I asked my sister a few days later. 'Now you're talking', she responded enthusiastically. I had to convince the three members of the leadership team. They were equally enthusiastic and gave me their blessing. Everything fell into place for me to volunteer with Solidarity with South Sudan, an inter-congregational initiative that was training teachers and midwives in this needy country.

It was three exhausting weeks of travel and all-day training session with young men and women learning to be midwives in the town of Wau; two sessions with seminarians in Juba and another session with staff of the Catholic radio station in Juba. Sr Cathy Arata, SND, the coordinator of Solidarity was my companion and guide. She made all the arrangements, raised the funds and drove me to venues in Juba. Fr Joseph, an Indian priest who ran the Solidarity guest house in Juba, was equally helpful. I was deeply impressed by their community spirit and by their perseverance in spite of the difficulties in a country with so few resources and a long history of violence. Cathy was also celebrating her Golden Jubilee that year so we were treated to a Jubilee Mass at the nearby Church and a delicious feast with many priests and sisters who attended. I felt at home and began to consider returning to work in South Sudan when I completed my term in leadership.

When I came back from this grueling but uplifting experience, I found Mary Ellen's health had declined. She was having more difficulty breathing and walking and started to use Access A Ride, a free transport system for the sick and elderly, to go to Sunday Mass and to see the doctor. I joined her and Barrett for Thanksgiving and arrived the night before. She was in bed after having a terrible day of gasping for breath. She kept calling her doctor to get her prescription changed back to a more expensive medication. He never picked up nor did his answering service.

On Thanksgiving morning, she felt a little better and joined me in the living room for a cup of tea. We made a few phone calls – to our Aunt Ruth Casey who was like a second mother to us, to a cousin in California and to my sister's former co-worker and good friend, Marianne Mocarski. She then stood up and used a walker to go to the bathroom. I helped her to walk and to carry her oxygen tank. As I stood at the doorway, I saw that she was struggling to breath. She looked at the oxygen monitor on her finger and it had plummeted to the 60s. I called Barrett who was in the bedroom. 'We need to call 911', I urged in desperation. Mary Ellen shook her head no. The numbers kept going down on the monitor. Barrett took the phone and made the call. Within minutes the para-medics arrived. They immediately gave her an injection and put her on a stretcher to go to a nearby hospital in an ambulance. Barrett and I followed, praying all the way that she would survive.

She spent the next week in an emergency ward in this hospital in Brooklyn that has since closed. The doctors and nurses were amazing – kind, helpful and professional. Most of them were immigrants. They came from India or Jamaica. She was then transferred to a ward in the same hospital to regain her strength and increase her lung capacity. Barrett and I spent long hours with her, marveling at her resilience and her humor. She loved to tell the story of how she wrestled with a doctor who tightened the breathing mask on her face so she felt that she was suffocating. 'I grabbed his tie and pulled him down until he loosened the straps. He won't forget me in a hurry', she laughed. We laughed with her.

The hospital suggested that she needed to move to a nursing home to recuperate. She asked me if she could come to the infirmary at Maryknoll. It broke my heart to say no. 'We don't have the necessary oxygen nor do we have staff who are qualified to treat respiratory diseases', I explained. 'It's so far away that it will be difficult for Barrett and your friends to visit'. While all these were true, I felt like I was betraying her by refusing to welcome her to our health facility.   The sister in charge of our nursing home came to the rescue. She knew the head of Mary Manning Walsh residence in Manhattan. It was run by the Ursulines and was on the upper east side near a subway line. The sister in charge agreed and Mary Ellen was transferred to a lovely private room not far from the nursing station. Barrett sat by her side every day and I came into the city when I could. Friends and relatives visited and brought her gifts, flowers and much needed distraction from the fact that she was not improving.

It soon became apparent that she could not do the occupational therapy that had been recommended. The therapist tried her best. 'I am making her suffer', she said sadly as she told us she was going to discontinue the treatment. Barrett and I accompanied Mary Ellen to her lung specialist who was just a block away from Mary Manning. He had an excellent reputation and taught at the nearby university. He rushed into the room where we were waiting and told us he only had a short time as he had a class waiting. To me it seemed that he had not bothered to read the charts from the hospital and asked Mary Ellen insulting questions. I dared to ask him what more could be done. He glared at me. 'You might consider a lung transplant', he said before leaving us with his assistant.

She was kind and considerate. When Mary Ellen said that she was scared, the young intern replied. 'Of course, you are scared. You have a life-threatening disease. It would be unusual if you weren't afraid'. We pushed Mary Ellen through the rain drops in her wheelchair back to her room at Mary Manning with little hope. The next day, however, my sister was optimistic and excited. When her friends Marge and Barbara came in, she had them look up information about lung transplants on their iPads and also started to look for equipment that she could use at home to help her live more comfortably. It was the best day since she had collapsed at home on Thanksgiving.

When I returned the following day, however, her mood had changed. 'A lung transplant might give me a few more months', she explained. 'Or even a few more years but then I would be back in the same situation'. She knew she was dying. She would not resist. I was still convinced that somehow a magic cure would be found or that my prayers and that of our sisters would produce a miracle. On New Year's Eve, she called her Pax Christi group on the phone. Each of them shared their prayer for the new year. When it was her turn, she said simply: 'I pray for peace. I pray for acceptance'. I left her room with tears streaming down my face.

I was now staying at the apartment of good friends, the Roses, on 34th St on the east side. Each morning I would take the bus up First Avenue and get off at 78th street to walk to the nursing home. I would stay with Mary Ellen until about 8:00 p.m. when she was ready to sleep. In the evenings I worked on my speech for the opening of the centennial of the Maryknoll Sisters on the feast of the Epiphany, January 6. When I thought the speech was ready, I read it to my sister. She listened intently and commented that it had some good points. Without criticizing or making me defensive, she made a suggestion: 'You know how those black preachers that you appreciate capture their listeners?' she asked. 'I can't be dramatic like them', I protested before she had finished. She continued as if I had not interrupted. 'They find a word or a phrase that captures the message and repeat it over and over. What is special about Maryknoll Sisters? What is the message of your founding?'

With these questions and suggestions ringing in my head, I went back to the apartment that night and started over. I reread the story of our founding with Mary Josephine Rogers. She told us in subsequent anniversaries that the first group of three women to come to Hawthorne, NY, 'followed their star to Maryknoll' as the three wise men had followed the star to Bethlehem. I had my word or phrase – the star - the star that led each of us to become missioners with Maryknoll. I then found some words from Archbishop Desmond Tutu that he had written about us for the revised edition of **Hearts on Fire**. These words spoke of what made us stand out, what defined our spirit. I quoted him. When I read the new version to Mary Ellen the next day, she smiled and said, 'You have captured it now'.

With this encouragement, I overcame my fear as I ascended the podium at Maryknoll on January 6, 2012 and proclaimed my brief opening words to the newly appointed Cardinal of NY, Timothy Dolan, to the family members of Mother Mary Joseph who were present and to all the sisters and friends who had assembled in the chapel for this anniversary. I will never forget the thrill of that day and the help of my sister who was nearing the end of her life.

At the beginning of each year, Mary Ellen threw a party for her friends. This year was no exception. She invited them to her room at Mary Manning and welcomed each one, thanking them for their friendship and kindness and for the food they had brought to celebrate with her and each other. I was entertaining the friends of Maryknoll on the opening of our centennial year while Mary Ellen entertained her dearest and most faithful friends and colleagues. She declined quickly after this celebration. At the end of the month, she transferred herself back to the hospital. Barrett, her best friend Marianne Mocarski and I were with her when the lung specialist arrived. 'What more can we do', she asked. He shrugged and suggested they could try a new medication. My sister looked at us and said, 'It's time for hospice'. The doctor turned away abruptly and left the three of us in tears. His assistant who was with him, gave us encouragement. 'Hospice is a good alternative and Calvary has a good reputation', she said. I was grateful for her presence and her understanding.

We fetched the social worker and everything moved quickly after that. The next day Mary Ellen was moved to the hospice section of the Lutheran hospital in Brooklyn. She received the last rites from a Nigerian priest who was chaplain there and said good-by to some friends who had come to Boston to see her. Mary Ellen was agitated, however, and asked to see the doctor. 'This isn't working', she wrote on a piece of paper as she could no longer speak. The doctor said that whatever my sister wanted would be done the following day when the regular doctor was there. It was a Sunday and this doctor was only a substitute. I wasn't sure what my sister meant and it was becoming difficult to communicate as she had an oxygen mask over her face and could not easily speak. The medication was also making her drowsy and she would doze from time to time.

Marianne, Barrett and I realized that the end was near and set up a rotating schedule so that Mary Ellen would never be alone, starting the following day. Barrett and Marianne left together about 7:00 p.m. after assuring Mary Ellen that she had the button to call the nurse or doctor at any time. We even laughed as she made a joke about the call button. I asked her if she would like some ice cream and was delighted when she said yes. When I found the cart and brought it back, she lifted the mask and took a few bites. She then put her hands across her chest, shut her eyes and fell asleep. I had never seen her so peaceful in the last two months. I stayed for another hour and then got the bus and subway back to the apartment on 34th St. I woke at about 3 a.m. and couldn't get back to sleep. About 6 a.m., I called the hospice nurse to see how she was. 'She died peacefully about 3 a.m.', she said. 'When we went to check on her, she was gone'. I fell to the floor, crying and screaming. My friends came running from the bedroom to comfort me. When I phoned Barrett, he said they had called him in the middle of the night but he was waiting for morning before he called me.

My sister Mary Ellen faced her death with faith and courage. 'I'm not afraid to die', she told me. 'But I fear *how* I might die'. Each time that her oxygen tank ran low, she faced the possibility of suffocation, her deepest fear. The hospice nurse assured us that she died peacefully as her heart and breathing slowed down and then stopped while she slept.

The long vigil was over.   Her wake and funeral were just what she would have wanted. Her funeral at St Barnabas, the church that she attended faithfully was meaningful and inspiring. The church was packed with many friends, neighbors and colleagues as well as many of our relatives who had come from California, Washington state and Pittsburgh, including our aunt Ruth Casey who was approaching ninety, and had driven to Brooklyn with two of her daughters and her daughter in law. The priest, Fr Anthony Andreassi, gave a moving homily using the text from Matthew 25, 'I was thirsty, hungry, naked, in prison and you cared for me', to describe her vocation as a social worker who cared about each child who came to Good Shepherd and their parents, who were often damaged and traumatized from their own upbringing. She never judged or blamed them but tried to understand and to restore their dignity and sense of self-worth. Barrett hosted a luncheon at their apartment after the service. This was the first time that most of my cousins had been there. They admired the mural on the rooftop that Tony Schaub, our artist cousin, had painted. He also painted a delightful mural on the ceiling of the bathroom in the apartment.

Suzy Schaub, our cousin from Mill Valley, CA, stayed for a few extra days to help Barrett and me sort through Mary Ellen's things and decide what to do with her beautiful clothing, jewelry, purses and scarves. We selected something for each of the women relatives and packed it and sent it to them. Suzy took Barrett and me out to supper that evening where we shared memories of Mary Ellen. I doubt if I could have done any of this without Suzy's support and encouragement.

When I returned to my hilltop home at Maryknoll after it was all over, Bernice Rigney, our personnel director and the friend who had accompanied me to Africa many years ago, suggested that I get away for a week to process my grief and pain at this tremendous loss. I agreed with her that I needed time to go over it all, to break down and cry in order to heal. We choose Emmaus House on the Jersey shore and Bernice drove me there a few days after the funeral. After we arrived, I walked down to the water and let the steady lap of the waves sooth my pain. As the wind buffeted me, a single sea gull swooped down and circled around me several times before flying off to sea. 'Thank you, Mary Ellen,', I whispered. 'Now I know you are flying free with no more fear of suffocating'.

27

The Road Less Traveled

'...Two roads diverged in a wood, and I –
I took the one less traveled by,
And that has made all the difference.'
Robert Frost

Not many young women took the road to religious life, even back in the 1950s and early 1960s when vocations to be sisters, brothers and priests flourished. From an early age, however, I knew that I wanted something different from my parents and my classmates; something perhaps more exciting, more heroic. I grew up in a Catholic environment, reading the lives of the saints and wanting to follow their example, to death if necessary! I was faithful to the practices and devotions of the Church together with my mother and my sister. We prayed the rosary on our knees each evening accompanied by the soaring voice of Bishop Fulton Sheen, a well-known radio and TV personality who made the doctrines of the church understandable to ordinary Catholics and non-Catholics alike. With my vivid imagination and dreams of becoming a saint and martyr, it is not surprising that I was attracted to religious life.

The Dominican Sisters were wonderful educators and role

models but I was not drawn to teaching in a local school. I dreamt of 'fields afar' where intrepid explorers and missionaries encountered exotic and dangerous cultures, so different from the very narrow and safe world in which I grew up. My reading of international authors fed my imagination with images of lands awaiting my arrival and fulfilling a longing in me to make a difference in the world. 'This is the life for me,' I thought when I saw photos of sisters riding on horseback through remote mountain villages in Guatemala or living on a houseboat on the Beni River in Bolivia. Sister Maria del Rey Danforth, the author of these marvelous missionary odysseys, had been a reporter with the Pittsburgh Press before she joined the Maryknoll Sisters and she knew how to tell a gripping tale.

I was probably not aware of the symbiotic relationship between colonialism and the Christian missionary enterprise, nor the destruction of cultures that resulted. Instinctively perhaps, I embraced diversity and admired the variety of languages and cultures on other continents. I had a collection of dolls from around the world. Each year great Aunt Catherine would give me one more to add to my display. This wide interest has been a constant in my life. I was certain my parents would support me in my decision to become a missionary sister.

I never looked back. Although, as mentioned above, I found some of the medieval practices in our training bizarre, I believed they were meant to toughen us and prepare us for a rigorous life. I was somewhat superstitious, believing that if I turned back, I would suffer the fate of Lot's wife who was turned into a pillar of salt for looking back at the destruction of Sodom and Gomorrah! This warning, crazy in retrospect, found fertile ground in my imagination and helped me persevere when others were leaving.

The thought of marriage and children could never compete with my glorified notion of being a missionary to distant lands, preferably to Africa. Although my parents' marriage had not been ideal, they showered Mary Ellen and me with love and trust and gave us freedom to choose our own path. Before my father died, I overhead my mother saying to him: 'Paul, whatever went wrong between us we did right by our girls.' My father nodded yes and smiled.

As recounted in previous chapters, the reality of mission life lived up to and exceeded my expectations. I enjoyed language school and picked up Swahili without much effort. I was excited to be spreading mass communications to every diocese in Kenya and contributing articles to Kenyan newspapers and magazines as well as drafting some of the pastoral letters for the bishops. Being fairly young and not wearing a religious habit had its advantages among my Protestant colleagues and the media personalities with whom I worked at the local radio and TV station as well as the press. 'You're a nun,' they would say, 'but you don't look like one.' While this broke through barriers, it also led to embarrassing encounters. One of the staff at the Voice of Kenya (VOK), for instance, persisted in making passes at me and I was often groped on the crowded buses that I would take into the city. I told the women at the VOK about the unwanted advances and I had no trouble after that but I did not know how to support the lay women at the Catholic Secretariat who came to me with their tales of sexual harassment by some of the local priests. I considered telling the bishops but doubted if my voice would be heard. I stayed silent.

In the midst of this involved life, the time came to decide whether to make my final commitment (vows) to this way of life. We had nine years after our first profession to make up our minds. I struggled with what I wanted to do with the rest of my life. I felt satisfied in my work but wondered if it was time for me to explore other roads. 'Take a leap into the unknown,' a male friend urged. I clung on the precipice, undecided until the very last minute. I made a retreat at Lumbwa, a Cistercian monastery set in the rolling hills of central Kenya. We woke up with the dawn to attend the chanting of the monks in the chapel and during the day I sat on the hillside pondering my decision. The beauty of nature surrounding me seeped into my spirit. 'I cannot say yes for the rest of my life but only for today,' I vowed. From that moment I was satisfied with a daily yes to my commitment.

We could devise our own vow formula at that time of experimentation. I chose to paraphrase some words from the renowned Brazilian educator Paulo Freire:

> *Lord Jesus, as you celebrate your entry into our world and into our lives, I, wishing to follow your example, give my whole life to you, in service to others. Desiring to participate more fully in (man's) struggle for liberation, and in the creation of a more human, (just and loving) world, I reaffirm my commitment to a celibate life, in community according to your Gospel and the demands of missionary service as a Maryknoll Sister.*

I celebrated the ceremony in June 1972 with our sisters in Kitale, Kenya, where they had a rural clinic. I could not face a big ceremony in Nairobi where I would have had to invite many people. Instead, this was a small event with about 12 of our sisters from Kenya and Tanzania. Bishop John Njenga, who had been the Secretary General at the Catholic Secretariat during my first years there, received my vows and seemed to enjoy the simplicity as much as I did. This public profession of vows solidified my desire to continue with my religious vocation although it did not eliminate future doubts and indecision.

I tended to view marriage and domestic life as a prison for women. The title of Maya Angelou's autobiographical story, I Know Why a Caged Bird Sings, struck a chord with me. My mother kept singing but lost much of her own melody; my father's voice was also distorted as my parents struggled to bridge the vast differences between them. I also heard the tearful tales of Kenyan and Zimbabwean women who shared their stories of domestic abuse and infidelity with me. When I considered changing paths, it was not for marriage and family life but for a political career, perhaps as a member of Congress in the United States, working with an international organization such as the United Nations, becoming a human rights lawyer or a journalist for a reputable newspaper. I never seriously explored these roads, however, as I was basically content in my vocation and able to do many of the same things that I could have done as a single independent woman.

I was interested in politics from as far back as I can remember. The different social background of my parents made me aware of inequality from an early age. My father introduced me to the exploitation of the working class and the need for workers like himself to organize to gain their rights while my mother showed me by example how to treat all people with respect. The Mayor of Pittsburgh, David Lawrence, was a neighbor. He was the first to get a TV at his home and invited all the children in the neighborhood to come and watch a popular children's program, Howdy Dowdy, on our way home from school. My mother played bridge with the daughters of our city councilor and was well informed about local issues. From childhood, therefore, I saw the importance of political involvement to bring about positive social and economic change.

Maryknoll enhanced this budding awareness of the causes of inequality and added an international dimension to my understanding. I learned tools of social analysis and participated in a group that looked at various US industries, such as the media, to trace the ownership and the interlocking links between various corporations. With Paulo Friere, I learned to trace the root causes of poverty by asking the simple question – why. 'Why don't you come to school?' 'Because I have no shoes.' 'Why do you have no shoes?' 'Because my father lost his job.' 'Why did he lose his job?' 'Because the company where he worked was bought out by another.' Why, why, why?

As I approach the close of these reflections, I recall that when we completed our six years in leadership, we were encouraged to have a time of renewal. I visited Ireland and fell instantly in love with this misty, magical green isle. My retreat at Glendalough, the Valley of Two Lakes, introduced me to St Kevin, who founded a monastery there in the sixth century and like St Francis, made friends with the birds and beasts, including a dragon that lived in the lake! The family of Lawrence O'Toole is buried at Glendalough and I finally learned the true story of Lawrence and not the one we were told at school. This Lawrence, who died in 1180, was the first Irish Archbishop of Dublin and very influential until the British no longer wanted him there.

I found my grandmother's birthplace in a small village in Galway, Cartoor. She was Mary Connolly. I had not expected to get so emotional but Mary became more than a grandmother to me as I traced my roots. I could imagine her as a teenager boarding a ship to the States on her own. As described earlier in the chapter on my roots, she disembarked at Ellis Island in 1904 and went to live with her Uncle Leo in Braddock, PA, just around the corner from the steel mills.

My last ministry before leaving Zimbabwe in May 2020 was in combatting human trafficking with the African Forum for Catholic Social Teaching (AFCAST) at Arrupe Jesuit University. I found it one of the most enriching experiences of my life. Gogo (Grandma) was my new name as I came to know and respect the courage and resilience of each of the women who had been trafficked to Kuwait. Getting to know and work side by side with survivors of trafficking was the highlight of my sixty years as a Maryknoll Sister.

None of these steps along the road was organized or planned by me. Rather, like St Paul at Damascus, I was constantly thrown from my horse and shown the way to go. While I was influenced by racist attitudes and structures in the United States, I have not lost my belief in the possibility of creating a non-racial society of equals where the color of the skin will not matter. I look back with gratitude at the rich journey and on the people who have opened my eyes to see the world through a new lens. Each step has made a difference in my life. 'I took the road less travelled by and that has made all the difference!'

On the African continent, I learned the importance of naming. Most children are named not only after a relative, usually a deceased grandparent, but also after an important event at the time of their birth or a trait that their parents wished for them such as Charity, Knowledge or Beauty. There are hundreds of Kennedys, named after the first US President to visit Africa where he was much admired. There are also children named Bush after the President who authorized the free distribution of antiretroviral drugs, a huge help to reduce death from AIDS. Children may be named after the month they were born or something that was happening at that time. Nhamo, hardship, is a common name during a time of drought or war. Forgiveness is also common indicating the need for harmony in the family. When I lived in Kenya, the people gave me the name, Nguthie, butterfly. This was appropriate for me since at that time I was flitting from one project to another and constantly on the move.

The butterfly is also a symbol of the resurrection. Having held the hand of each of my parents as they peacefully took their last breath, I could not doubt that they had been born to a new life. As I stood at the bedside of countless men and women in Zimbabwe who suffered and died from AIDS, I witnessed a freedom in letting go of the pain and embracing the mystery of death. I saw this same freedom and even joy in the passing of many of our senior Sisters who had given their lives to helping others.

I will always treasure his revolutionary statement that the color of the skin doesn't matter. Although I realized that this was an ideal that would be difficult to achieve, that vision of a 'color-blind' world may have prevented the slaughter of whites in Zimbabwe. It may also have prevented racial hostility after Independence. It is a mantra that is sorely needed in my home country, the United States, where racism remains strong in spite of the fact that the majority of voters elected an African-American President, twice.